A Williamson **KIDS CAN!** Book

Paper Folding Fun!

DATE DUE

50 Awesome Crafts to Weave, Twist & Curl

Ginger Johnson

Illustrations by Betsy Day

Williamson Publishing W Charlotte, Vermont

P9-BHT-978

Copyright © 2002 by Ginger Johnson

All rights reserved.

No portion of this book may be reproduced mechanically, electronically, or by any other means including photocopying or on the Internet without written permission of the publisher.

Library of Congress Cataloging-in-Publication Data

Johnson, Ginger, 1946-
   Paper-folding fun! : 50 awesome crafts to weave, twist & curl / Ginger Johnson.
      p. cm. — (A Williamson kids can! book)
   Includes index.
   Summary: Provides step-by-step instructions for creating fifty paper crafts, including pop-up greeting cards, stacking boxes, folded journals, and three-dimensional creatures, plus "magic" paper tricks.
   ISBN 1-885593-67-8 (pbk.)
   1. Paper work—Juvenile literature. [1. Paper work. 2. Handicraft. 3. Magic tricks.] I. Title. II. Series.

TT870 .J64 2002
745.54—dc21

2002016825

Kids Can!® series editor: **Susan Williamson**
Project editor: **Vicky Congdon**
Interior design: **Nancy-jo Funaro**
Illustrations: **Betsy Day**
Cover design: **Marie Ferrante-Doyle**
Front cover photography: **Peter J. Coleman**
Back cover photography: **Sarah Rakitin**
Printing: **Capital City Press**

Williamson Publishing Co.
P.O. Box 185
Charlotte, VT 05445
(800) 234-8791

Manufactured in the United States of America

10 9 8 7 6 5 4 3 2 1

Kids Can!®, Little Hands®, Kaleidoscope Kids®, and Tales Alive!® and are registered trademarks of Williamson Publishing.

Good Times™, Quick Starts for Kids!™, and You Can Do It!™ are trademarks of Williamson Publishing.

Notice: The information contained in this book is true, complete, and accurate to the best of our knowledge. All recommendations and suggestions are made without any guarantees on the part of the author or Williamson Publishing. The author and publisher disclaim all liability incurred in conjunction with the use of this information.

Dedication

In memory of
Virginia Janssen
and especially for
Chloe, Spencer, and Ethan.

Acknowledgments

Special thanks to my soul mate and husband, Eric, who happily understands and supports my need to create! Lots of thanks to our two sons, Andrew and Eric, and daughters-in-law, Tammy and Heather, for encouragement. Heaps of thanks to my talented sister, Judy, for her wisdom. Thanks to my father, Arthur Janssen, who, along with my artistic mother, taught me the happiness that comes with using one's hands to create. Without their constant support, this book would never have been written.

Many thanks to my editor, Vicky Congdon, and to the entire staff at Williamson Publishing for helping to make writing a book a joyous process.

And my special appreciation goes to Betsy Day, who transformed my projects with her wonderful artistic illustrations.

Over the years, close friends have encouraged me with my project-making activities in the arts. Thank you, Pat and Jerry, Sue and Dave, Chris and Danny, Ginny and Lowell, and Sue and Jim. A big hug of appreciation goes to my crafty pal, Terri.

I wish to thank Linda Lembke and Paul Johnson for their instruction, inspiration, and love of "the book arts."

Last, I wish to thank all of my students at Charlotte Central School, Charlotte, Vermont, for teaching me a love of learning and the joy of laughter.

The author is donating a portion of the proceeds from the sale of this book to the American Cancer Society.

Contents

Welcome to the Magical World of Paper Folding!

I always get excited when I unwrap a new package of paper — my imagination takes off in all directions! It never ceases to amaze me what I can make with a single piece of paper. With just one fold, you can create a mini-book, a pop-up card, a decorative fan, or a spiral book complete with a secret message! Add more folds, a few sequins or curls and ta-da! — it's a 3-D star, an elegant origami-bead necklace, a fire-spitting dragon, or a journal whose multicolored pages magically intertwine. But my real favorites are the mysterious paper creations that look impossible to duplicate — the ones with a trick fold that your friends beg you to show them. I'm still learning and mastering new folds!

I've gathered my paper-folding favorites for you here, along with other traditional paper crafts such as weaving and quilling. You'll have hours of fun making one-of-a-kind gifts, awesome party invites and favors, and cool room decorations. Try your hand at creating gorgeous paper jewelry, amazing handmade books and journals, and magical folds that will fool your friends. You'll find plenty to choose from when you're by yourself, looking for something special to do. Other projects are perfect for making with a friend or even a group of friends! With your imagination (and this book as a guide), there's no limit to your paper-folding adventures.

As a classroom teacher, one of the first things I do every fall is turn my students into paper-folding pros. So, let me turn you into a pro, too! Guaranteed!

Paper-Folding Supplies

At a Glance

These handy icons will help you choose a craft to make.

These crafts use basic, one-step folds. They are a great place to start if you have never done any origami or other paper-folding crafts.

These crafts are more involved, and use two-step folds. Some require making one or two separate sections and then assembling them to complete the craft.

These crafts are more challenging and require more patience. They have multi-step folds, as well as multi-step directions. For most of these crafts, you make several sections and then assemble them. The cutting is often more intricate, and the folds may be a little tricky, or simply require extra attention for precise results.

The most important supply: paper!

One of the most fun parts of making awesome paper crafts is picking the paper — there's so much to choose from! (I could write a book on my favorite papers alone!)

Check stationery shops, as well as school-, art-, and office-supply stores, for fantastic selections of paper — vivid colors, cool designs (on one side or both), even metallic finishes — to name a few. You can also recycle favorite cards, photos from magazines, and gift wrap into paper creations.

Paper comes in different weights. The thinner it is, the easier it is to fold, but make sure it's sturdy enough for your project. I recommend *card stock*, a medium-weight paper, for most of these crafts because it's easy to fold, holds up well, and comes in a wide range of wonderful bright colors. It's readily available in 8$\frac{1}{2}$" x 11" (21 x 27.5 cm) sheets; you'll find larger sizes at art-supply stores.

Be sure to store your collection of papers *flat*, in a drawer or a large box, for example. Under the bed is another good, out-of-the-way spot.

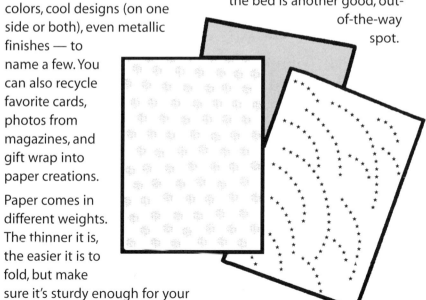

Bone paper folder or Popsicle stick

A *bone paper folder*, used in making

books, is one tool I highly recommend. It makes a firm, precise crease in the paper and is especially handy with medium- or heavy-weight papers. Available at art-supply stores, a small one costs $4 to $7.

You can also use a Popsicle stick (or even your thumbnail), but the paper may tear if you press too hard.

Scissors

For clean cuts, your scissors should be nice and sharp. A 7" or 8" (17.5 or 20 cm) blade is easiest to work with. (Don't "borrow" the fabric scissors out of the sewing box to cut your paper because it will dull them very quickly.)

You can also buy special scissors called *edgers* that make a decorative pattern as you cut borders and edges. They're fun to use and add a nice finishing touch to a project.

Craft knife

A *craft knife* (also called a *utility knife*) allows you to easily cut even strips of paper with a very clean edge. It is *very* sharp, however, so please get a grown-up to help you while using this tool, and be sure to protect your work surface with several layers of old newspaper or a piece of thick cardboard.

Ruler

It's handy to have both a 6" (15 cm) ruler for small projects and a 12" (30 cm) ruler for marking large pieces of paper. A metal ruler with a cork backing will make really accurate lines (the ruler doesn't slip).

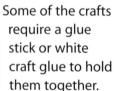

Glue

Some of the crafts require a glue stick or white craft glue to hold them together.

Toothpick, nail, or pencil

Handy for rolling or curling a strip of paper.

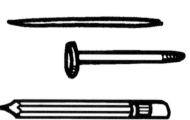

Decorating supplies

Use sequins, pom-poms, glitter, yarn, ribbon, stickers, beads, buttons, cutout photos, rubber stamps, markers, and gel pens to put the finishing touches on your paper creations. Look for hole punches with different-shaped holes like moons, stars, and flowers for jazzing up borders. You can also decorate with the little punched-out pieces, called *punch confetti.*

Tricks of the Trade

A fold that will hold

All the cool-looking paper crafts in this book — from the simplest to the most challenging — require one basic skill: making a perfect fold. That means a fold that is nice and straight, firmly creased, and has edges that line up perfectly! Often, it's the quality of the fold that holds a paper craft together and gives it its precise shape (a handmade box, for example) or allows you to unfold and refold it smoothly in a pleasing way.

It's always a good idea to practice a more advanced fold on a piece of scrap paper. If you're having trouble getting the hang of a particular fold, try it first on a lighter-weight paper.

Four steps to a perfect fold

These steps are the basis of any straight, crisp fold. Always start with a piece of paper that is evenly cut on all sides (see Cutting Tips, page 9).

1. **Match up the corners or sides** (depending on the fold called for in the instructions) carefully, and hold them firmly in place with the heel of your palm or your fingertips.

2. **Press down along the fold** with your fingers (it's usually easiest to use the hand you write with to make the fold).

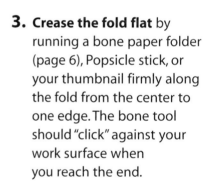

3. **Crease the fold flat** by running a bone paper folder (page 6), Popsicle stick, or your thumbnail firmly along the fold from the center to one edge. The bone tool should "click" against your work surface when you reach the end.

4. **Repeat** from the center to the other edge. Wow! Check out that nice, crisp fold!

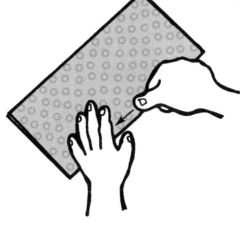

Scoring paper

It's easier to fold stiff or heavy-weight paper if you *score* the fold line first. This just means marking the fold line with an indent, which you'll use as a guide along which to fold.

Place a ruler on the paper where you want the fold to be. Draw the tip of a Popsicle stick or bone paper folder along the ruler, pressing down hard so that you leave a mark on the paper.

Cutting tips

The more carefully you cut, the nicer your finished craft will look. Try this technique for marking and cutting a straight edge on your paper. Let's say you need to cut a piece of paper that's 2" x 6" (5 x 15 cm):

1. Measure and mark 2" (5 cm) at the top and bottom of the paper and at several places along the length of the paper.

2. With the ruler, draw a line connecting those marks.

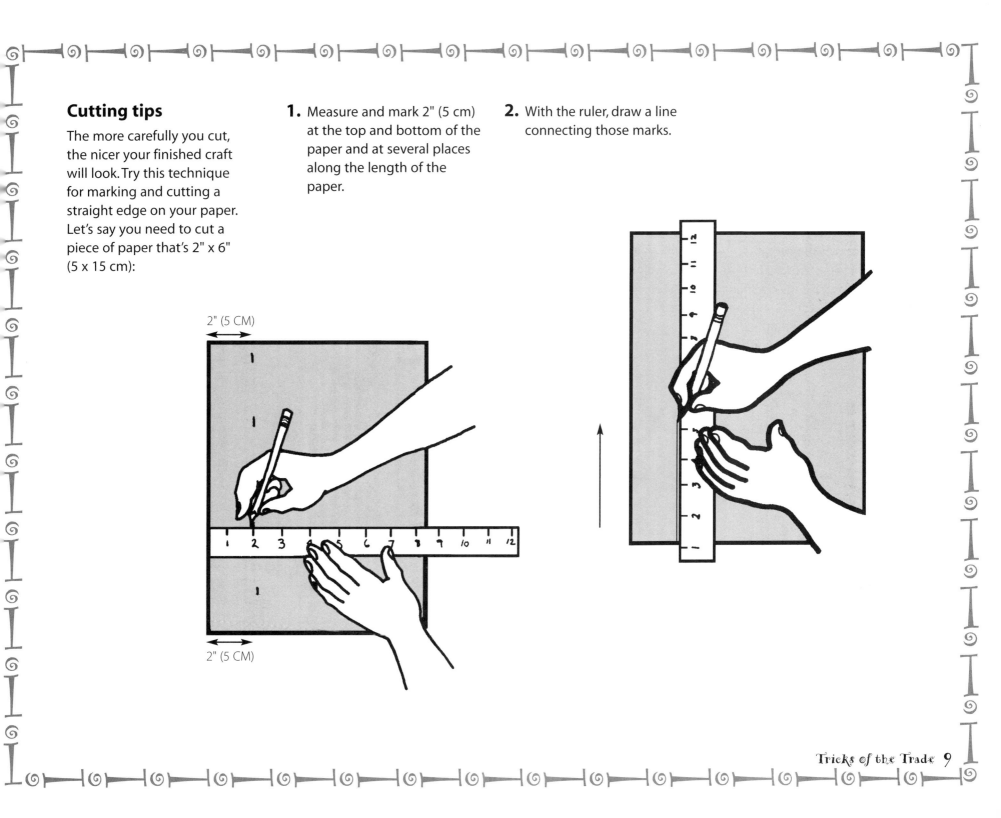

3. Cut along that line with either scissors or a craft knife (page 6).

4. Measure and mark off 6" (15 cm) on the strip. Connect those marks with ruler.

5. Cut along that line.

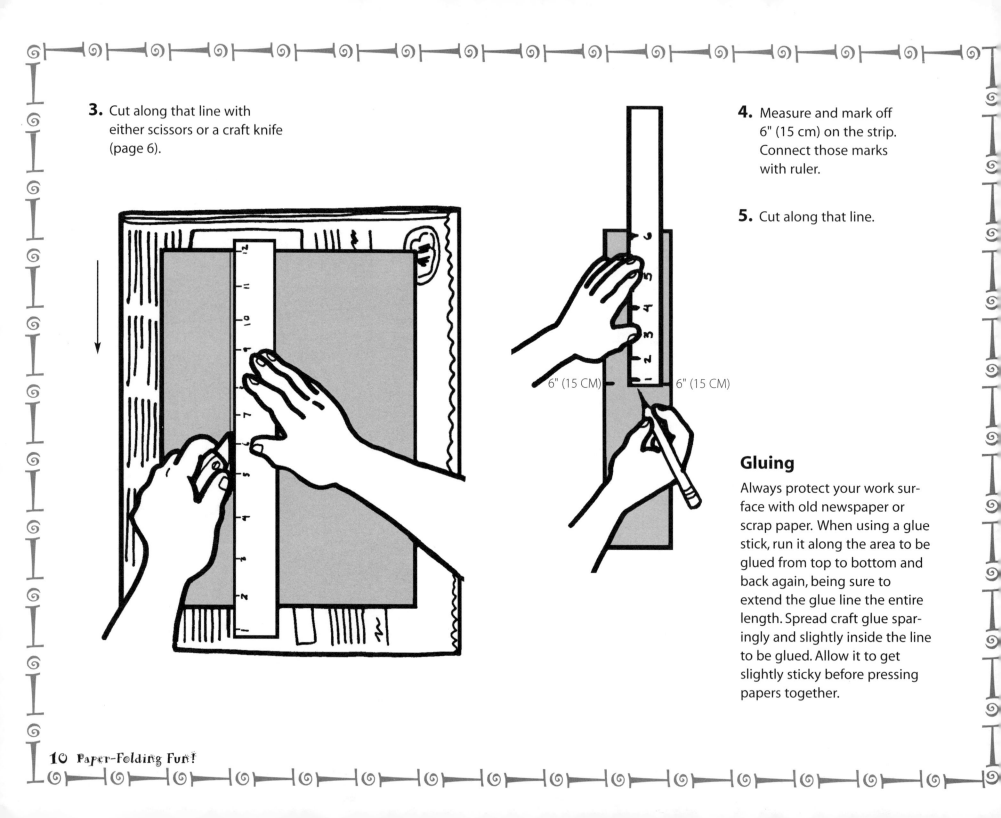

6" (15 CM)   6" (15 CM)

Gluing

Always protect your work surface with old newspaper or scrap paper. When using a glue stick, run it along the area to be glued from top to bottom and back again, being sure to extend the glue line the entire length. Spread craft glue sparingly and slightly inside the line to be glued. Allow it to get slightly sticky before pressing papers together.

The Amazing Accordion Fold

The cool cards, mini-books (from simple to intricate), and decorations in this chapter all start with the *accordion fold*. If you've ever seen an accordion, you know just what this fold looks like. You might think that to create it, you start at one end of the paper and fold back and forth, back and forth, but guess what? You'll end up with uneven sections and edges that don't line up. That's why there's an easy technique that a paper-folding pro (that's you!) uses to get a nice, tidy accordion with all the edges magically lined up! And once you know it, you can make some amazing creations!

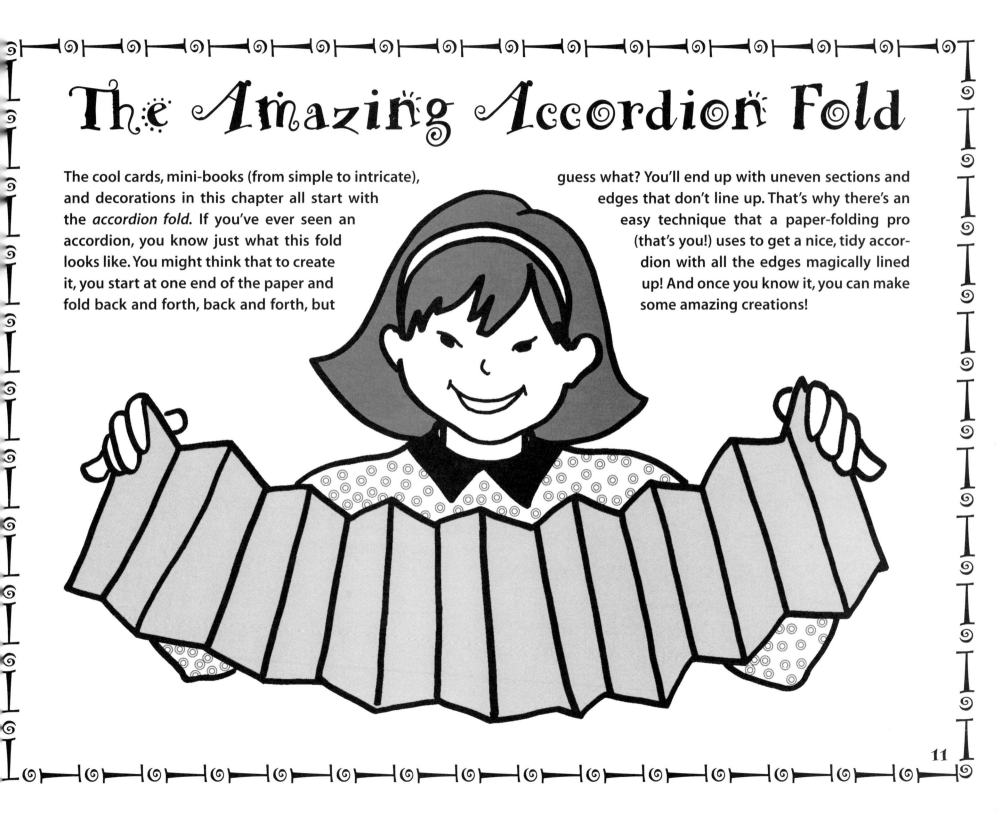

Making accordion folds

For the first three folds, you'll see your accordion shape right away. For the "square" folds, you'll need to make the cuts specified in the craft before you can fold the paper back and forth.

The four-panel accordion

1. With the paper as shown, fold (page 7) the paper in half, matching the short edges. Open the fold.

2. Bring the right edge of the paper to the center fold line. Crease the fold.

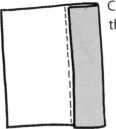

3. Bring the left edge of the paper to the center fold line. Crease the fold.

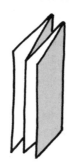

4. Reverse the center fold.

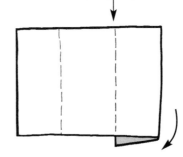

See how the folded sections stack up neatly? You have an exact rectangle with all the edges and folds lined up — your accordion fold is complete!

The eight-panel accordion

1. Make a four-panel accordion through step 3. Open the folds.

2. Reverse the right-hand fold.

CENTER FOLD

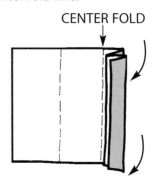

Open the fold. Bring the right-hand fold line to the center fold line; crease the fold.

CENTER FOLD

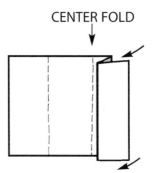

3. Bring the right edge to the center fold line.

CENTER FOLD

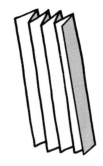

4. Repeat steps 2 and 3 on the left side. Reverse the center fold to complete the accordion fold.

The 16-panel accordion

1. Make the eight-panel accordion (page 12). Open all the folds.

2. Reverse the fold to the right of the center fold line.

CENTER FOLD

Open the fold. Bring that fold line to the center fold line; crease the fold.

CENTER FOLD

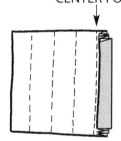

3. Bring the next right-hand fold line to the center fold line; crease the fold.

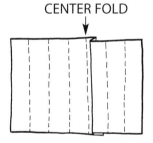

4. Reverse the last fold line; bring it to the center fold line.

CENTER FOLD

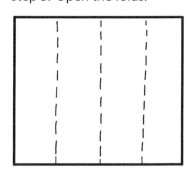

5. Fold the right edge to the center fold line; crease the fold.

CENTER FOLD

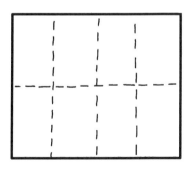

6. Repeat steps 2 through 5 on the left side. Reverse the center fold to complete the accordion fold.

The eight-square fold

1. Make the four-panel accordion (page 12) through step 3. Open the folds.

2. Fold the paper in half, matching the long edges. When you unfold it, you'll see eight sections.

The 16-square fold

1. Make an eight-square fold.

2. With the paper unfolded, bring the top (long) edge of the paper to the center fold line. Crease the fold. Open the fold.

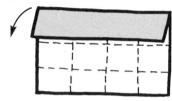

3. Bring the bottom (long) edge of the paper to the center fold line. Crease the fold.

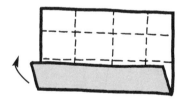

4. Open the fold. You now have 16 sections.

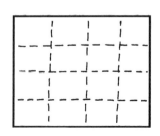

Four-Fold Accordion Book

It takes only a minute or two to make these four folds and — ta-da! — you've got a photo folder, a two-sided storybook, or a journal to record your adventures.

Decide how many pages you want and whether you want a cover (see MORE FOLDING FUN!, page 15) before you fill the pages.

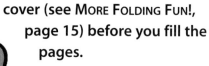

What you need

- Card stock, 4" x 18" (10 x 45 cm)
- Bone paper folder or Popsicle stick (page 6)
- Glue
- Paper, 3$\frac{1}{2}$" x 4" (8.5 x 10 cm), eight pieces in a contrasting color
- Markers or colored pencils
- Photos (optional)

What you do

1. With the card stock, make a four-panel accordion (page 12).

2. Glue one piece of the contrasting paper in the center of each square. If you are adding additional pages to your book (see MORE FOLDING FUN!, page 15), add them before completing this step.

3. Write messages on each page or alternate with drawings or photos.

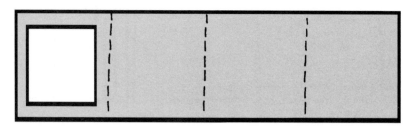

More Folding Fun!

Add more pages

1. Cut (page 9) a strip 4" x 18¹⁄₂" (10 x 46 cm).

2. With the strip as shown, score (page 8) a ¹⁄₂" (1 cm) line along the left edge and fold (page 7) this tab under.

¹⁄₂" (1 CM)

SCORE AND
FOLD UNDER

3. Fold the strip into a four-panel accordion (page12). Open the folds.

4. To attach, glue the tab of the new strip to the end page of the original accordion book.

GLUE TAB HERE

Finishing Touches

✸ **TO ADD A COVER,** trace around the closed book onto card stock. Cut out two matching pieces. Apply glue to the outsides of your book and press the covers in place. Tie your book closed with a colorful ribbon.

✸ **MAKE PHOTO HOLDERS** by cutting paper triangles large enough to cover the corners securely. Place the triangles just outside each picture and glue on the outside edges only, leaving the inside edge open.

GLUE HERE

✸ **JAZZ UP THE PAGES, BORDERS, AND COVER** with glitter glue, markers or gel pens, or a decorative paper punch or *punch confetti* (the little paper shapes that you punch out).

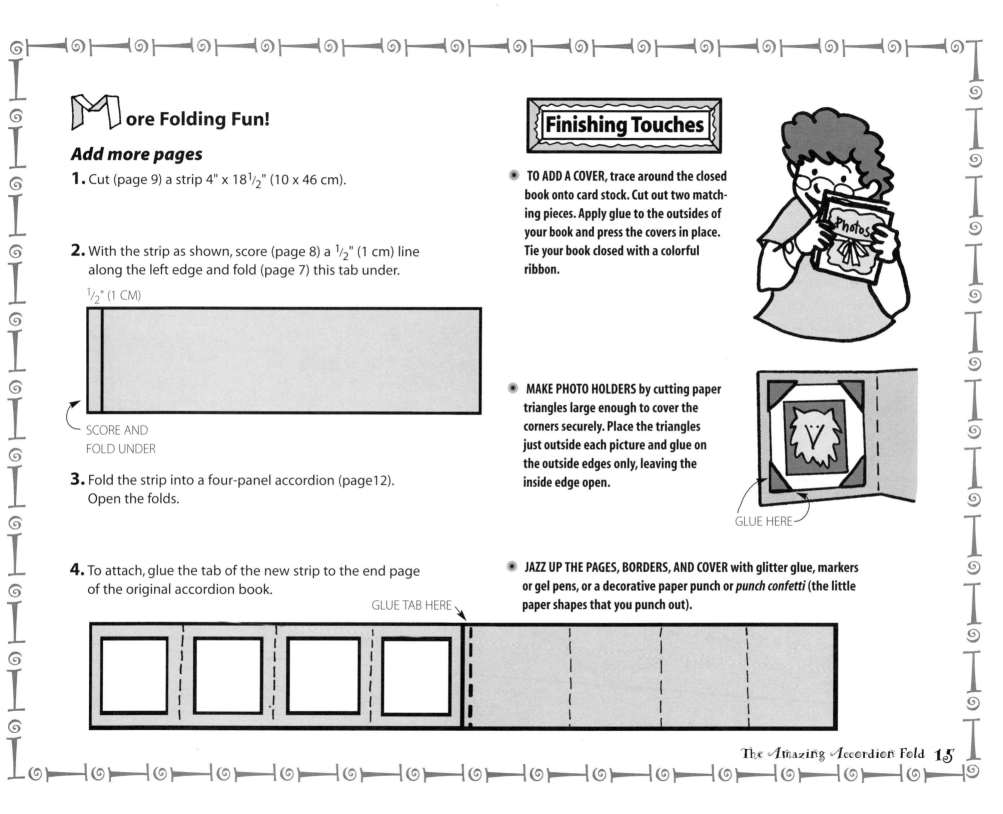

Accordion-Fold Book with Pockets

Organize stickers, small drawings or photos, or trip souvenirs in these handy pockets. It's also a super way to store small leftover pieces of special papers for your next paper-crafting project. Or, how about a sequence-of-events book report or an historical time line that will knock the teacher's socks off? Each pocket holds text and illustrations that you can easily remove to tell each section of the story. These instructions make a finished book that has 4¹⁄₂" x 9" (11 x 22.5 cm) sections with 3" (7.5 cm) pockets.

What you need

- Card stock, 12" x 18" (30 x 45 cm)
- Bone paper folder or Popsicle stick (page 6)
- Ruler
- Glue

What you do

1. With the card stock as shown, fold (page 7) the bottom edge up about 3" (7.5 cm). Open the fold.

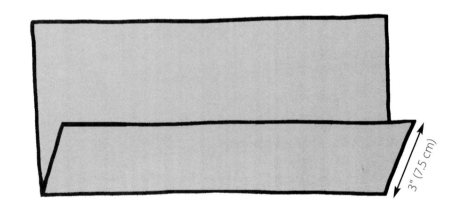

3" (7.5 cm)

2. Now, make a four-panel accordion (page 12). Open the folds.

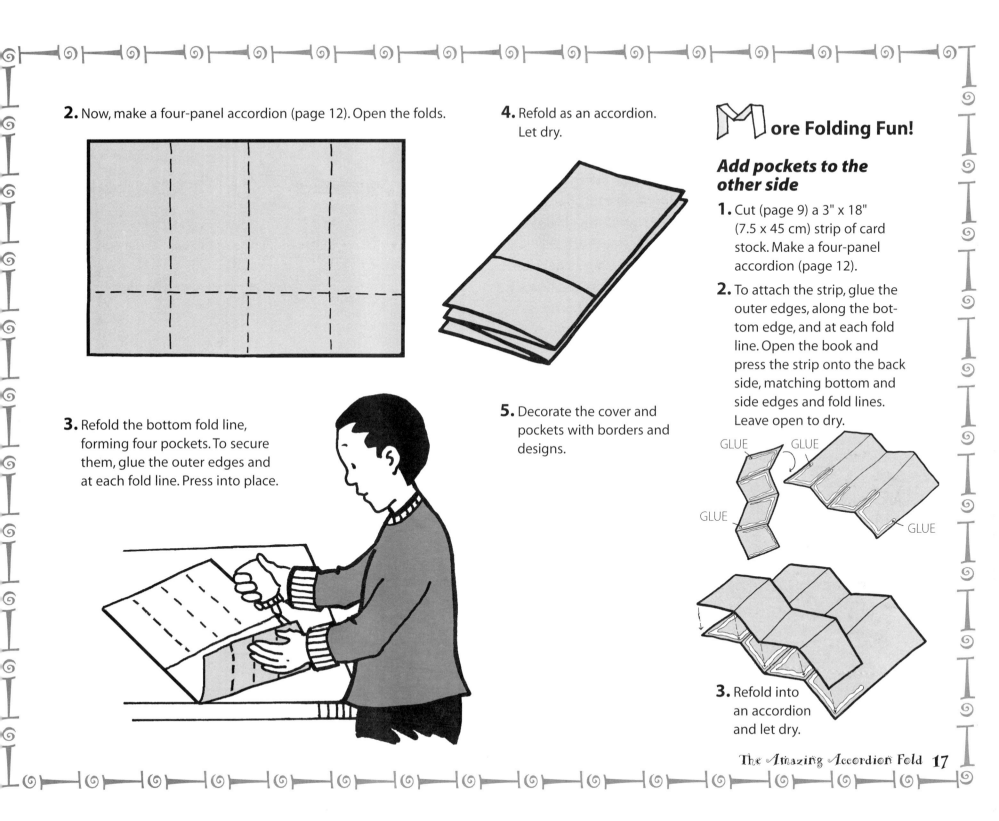

3. Refold the bottom fold line, forming four pockets. To secure them, glue the outer edges and at each fold line. Press into place.

4. Refold as an accordion. Let dry.

5. Decorate the cover and pockets with borders and designs.

More Folding Fun!

Add pockets to the other side

1. Cut (page 9) a 3" x 18" (7.5 x 45 cm) strip of card stock. Make a four-panel accordion (page 12).

2. To attach the strip, glue the outer edges, along the bottom edge, and at each fold line. Open the book and press the strip onto the back side, matching bottom and side edges and fold lines. Leave open to dry.

GLUE GLUE

GLUE

GLUE

3. Refold into an accordion and let dry.

The Amazing Accordion Fold **17**

Star-Fold Book Necklace

Create a piece of readable, wearable art! Start with the accordion fold, then with one simple snip, you've got a "star" that folds itself right into a little book. Present it on Mother's Day with a special message inside or create a cool birthday present for a friend.

If you like the "book look," check out the MINI-BOOK CHARM BRACELET (page 23). For another necklace style, see the MATCHBOX NECKLACE (page 105).

๕ what you need ๕

- Card stock:
  6" x 9" (15 x 22.5 cm) for the book;
  5" x 3$\frac{1}{4}$" (12.5 x 8 cm) for the cover
- Bone paper folder or Popsicle stick (page 6)
- Scissors
- Hole punch
- Yarn or ribbon, 24" (60 cm)

๕ what you do ๕

1. With the card stock, make an eight-square fold (page 13).

2. Fold the paper in half again, matching the short edges. Cut into that fold and along the horizontal center fold line to the next fold line.

FOLD LINE

CUT TO HERE

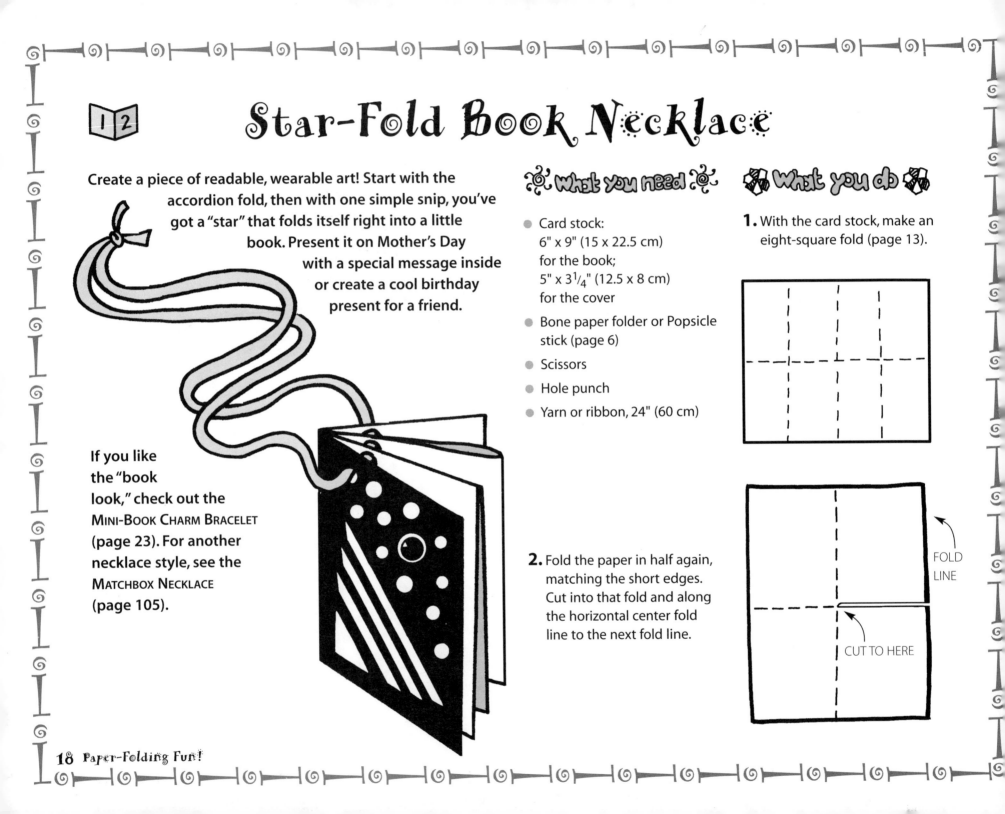

3. Open the fold. Hold the paper so that the vertical center fold is pointing up.

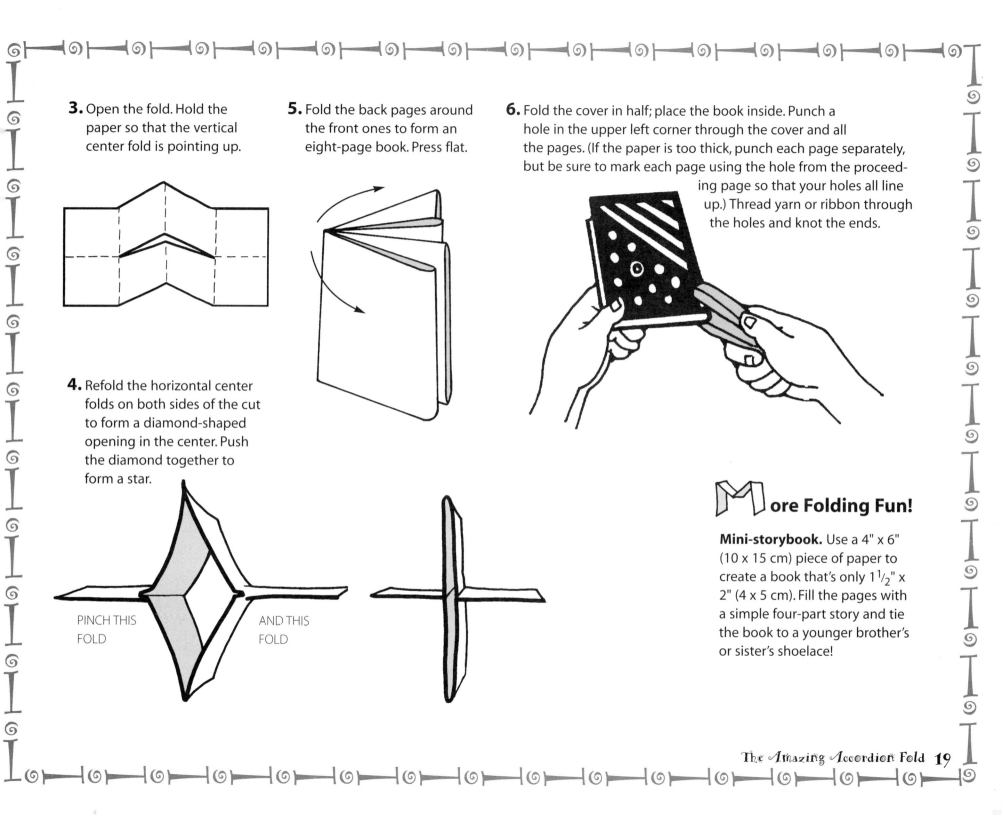

5. Fold the back pages around the front ones to form an eight-page book. Press flat.

6. Fold the cover in half; place the book inside. Punch a hole in the upper left corner through the cover and all the pages. (If the paper is too thick, punch each page separately, but be sure to mark each page using the hole from the proceeding page so that your holes all line up.) Thread yarn or ribbon through the holes and knot the ends.

4. Refold the horizontal center folds on both sides of the cut to form a diamond-shaped opening in the center. Push the diamond together to form a star.

PINCH THIS FOLD

AND THIS FOLD

More Folding Fun!

Mini-storybook. Use a 4" x 6" (10 x 15 cm) piece of paper to create a book that's only 1$\frac{1}{2}$" x 2" (4 x 5 cm). Fill the pages with a simple four-part story and tie the book to a younger brother's or sister's shoelace!

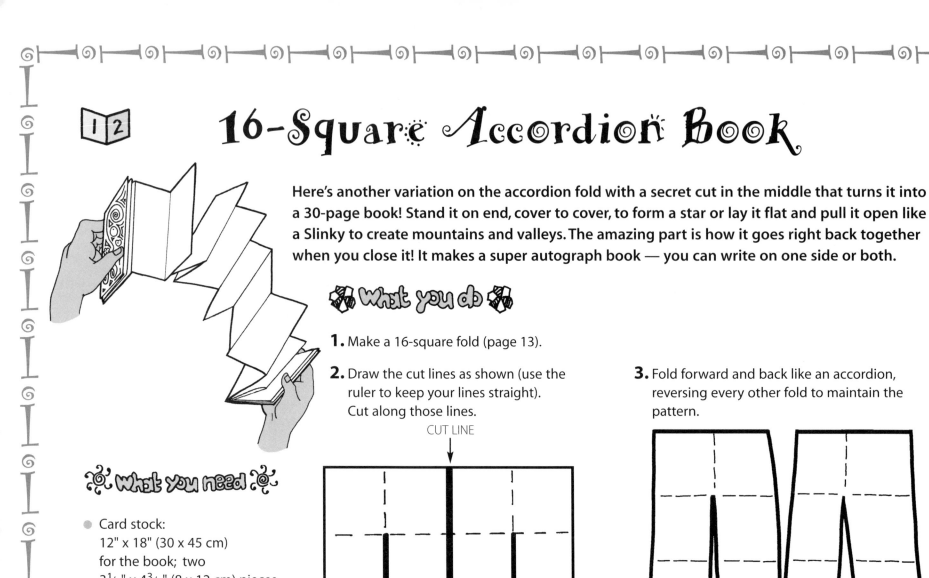

16-Square Accordion Book

Here's another variation on the accordion fold with a secret cut in the middle that turns it into a 30-page book! Stand it on end, cover to cover, to form a star or lay it flat and pull it open like a Slinky to create mountains and valleys. The amazing part is how it goes right back together when you close it! It makes a super autograph book — you can write on one side or both.

What you do

1. Make a 16-square fold (page 13).

2. Draw the cut lines as shown (use the ruler to keep your lines straight). Cut along those lines.

CUT LINE

CUT LINE   CUT LINE

3. Fold forward and back like an accordion, reversing every other fold to maintain the pattern.

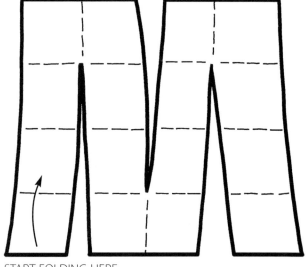

START FOLDING HERE

4. Glue the covers to the front and back pages.

What you need

- Card stock: 12" x 18" (30 x 45 cm) for the book; two 3$\frac{1}{4}$" x 4$\frac{3}{4}$" (8 x 12 cm) pieces for the cover
- Bone paper folder or Popsicle stick (page 6)
- Pencil
- Ruler
- Scissors

Finishing Touches

✳ **DECORATE THE INTERIOR PAGES** by gluing on squares of paper in contrasting colors (see step 2, page 14).

✳ **CHANGE THE PAPER DIMENSIONS** to create birthday cards or mini-books.

More Folding Fun!

Around-the-center cut

1. With the same size card stock, make a 16-square fold (page 13). Open the folds.

2. Cut out the center as shown.

CUT ON THESE LINES ↑

3. Fold forward and back like an accordion, reversing every other fold to maintain the pattern.

START FOLDING HERE ↑

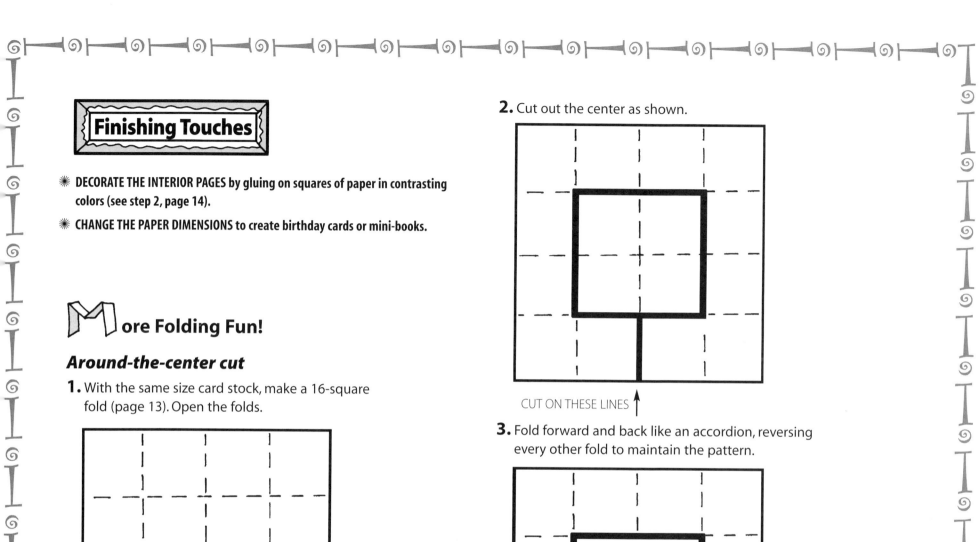

Decorative Mini-Fan

Hang this dangler in the window so it can twist in the breeze, or use it as a fancy shade pull. Or, make an assortment in different patterns and hang together for a mobile. It works best to use lightweight two-sided decorative paper (if using one-sided paper, glue two sheets together). For ornaments, use your favorite holiday gift wrap.

What you need

- Decorative paper, 4" x 8¹/₂" (10 x 21 cm)
- Bone paper folder or Popsicle stick (page 6)
- Narrow ribbon, 16" (40 cm)
- Glue

What you do

1. Make a 16-panel accordion (page 13).

2. Glue the folds together at one end to form a fan. Knot the ribbon around the fan base. Knot the free ends to create a loop, or tie them onto the pull cord of a shade.

More Folding Fun!

Make a mini-wheel!

1. With a 4" x 8¹/₂" (10 x 21 cm) piece of paper, make a 16-panel accordion (page 13).

2. Double-knot the ribbon at the center of the folded accordion.

3. Glue the top and bottom of one end panel and press together as shown, hiding the ribbon in the middle. Hold firmly until the glue sets. Repeat at the other end.

4. Tie the other ends of the ribbon in a bow.

GLUE TOGETHER

GLUE TOGETHER

 # Mini-Book Charm Bracelet

Make this tiny bracelet in the same decorative paper as the STAR-FOLD BOOK NECKLACE (page 18) or the MATCHBOX NECKLACE (page 105) for a matching set!

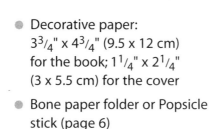 **what you need**

- Decorative paper: 3³/₄" x 4³/₄" (9.5 x 12 cm) for the book; 1¹/₄" x 2¹/₄" (3 x 5.5 cm) for the cover

- Bone paper folder or Popsicle stick (page 6)

- Glue

- Narrow ribbon, 12" (30 cm)

what you do

1. With the book paper, make the 16-SQUARE ACCORDION BOOK (page 20). If using one-sided decorative paper, fold decorative side to decorative side, followed by plain side to plain side to be sure the decorated side faces out when you fold it into a book.

2. Fold the cover in half, short sides together. Glue the insides and along the fold line. Lay the ribbon along the fold.

3. Place the folded book into the cover and press into place. Leave the book open to dry (so the pages don't stick together).

4. Size the bracelet to your wrist and knot the ends of the ribbon.

1 2 3 Stitched Surprise Card with Envelope

A few quick stitches attach the decorative pages of this card right into the fold, and it's easy to make an envelope to match. Then, fill the pages with poems, magazine pictures, or messages, and give to a special friend or relative!

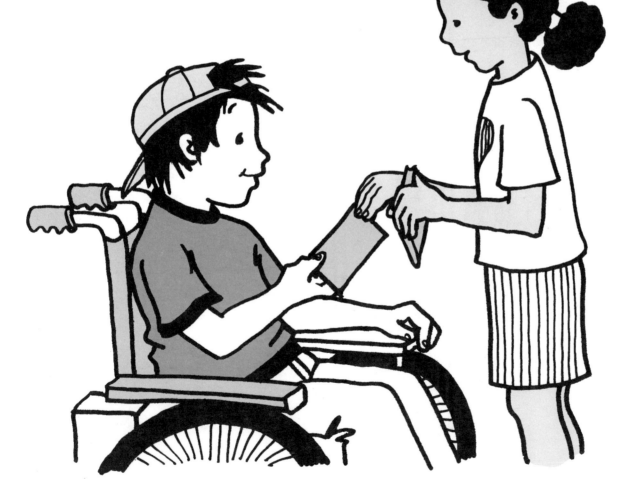

What you need

For the card:

- Card stock, 8¹/₂" x 11" (21 x 27.5 cm), in a solid background color
- Decorative paper, two 4" x 5¹/₄" (10 x 13 cm) pieces
- Bone paper folder or Popsicle stick (page 6)
- Edgers (page 6)
- Needle
- Thread
- Glue

For the envelope:

- Decorative paper, 5¹/₂" x 8¹/₂" (13.5 x 21 cm), in a matching or contrasting color

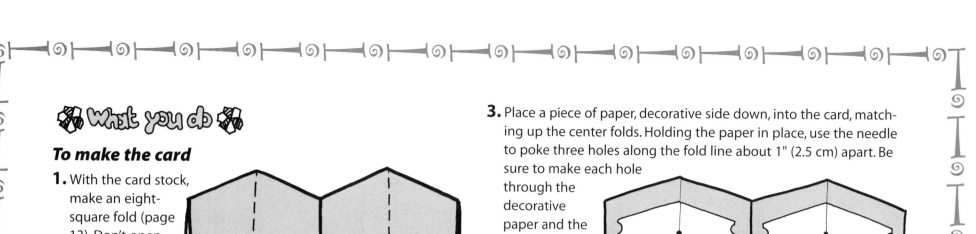

🎲 What you do 🎲

To make the card

1. With the card stock, make an eight-square fold (page 13). Don't open the final fold. Fold into an accordion, reversing folds as necessary.

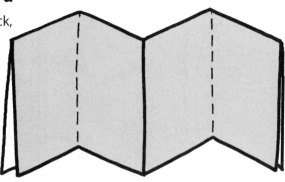

2. Fold each piece of decorative paper in half, matching the short sides. With the edgers, trim the short sides. Open the fold.

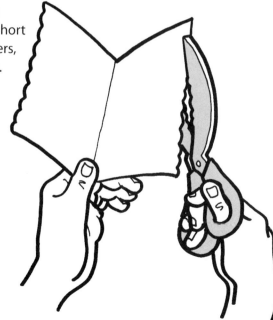

3. Place a piece of paper, decorative side down, into the card, matching up the center folds. Holding the paper in place, use the needle to poke three holes along the fold line about 1" (2.5 cm) apart. Be sure to make each hole through the decorative paper and the two layers of card stock.

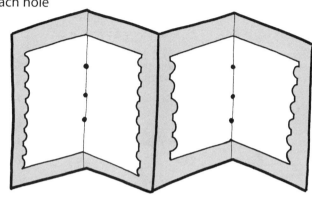

4. Thread the needle with a double strand and knot it. Stitch it to the card stock as shown.

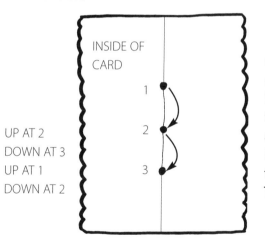

INSIDE OF CARD

UP AT 2
DOWN AT 3
UP AT 1
DOWN AT 2

1
2
3

On the outside of the card, knot the thread ends around the long stitch to secure it. Trim the ends.

5. Repeat steps 3 and 4 to attach the other decorative page.

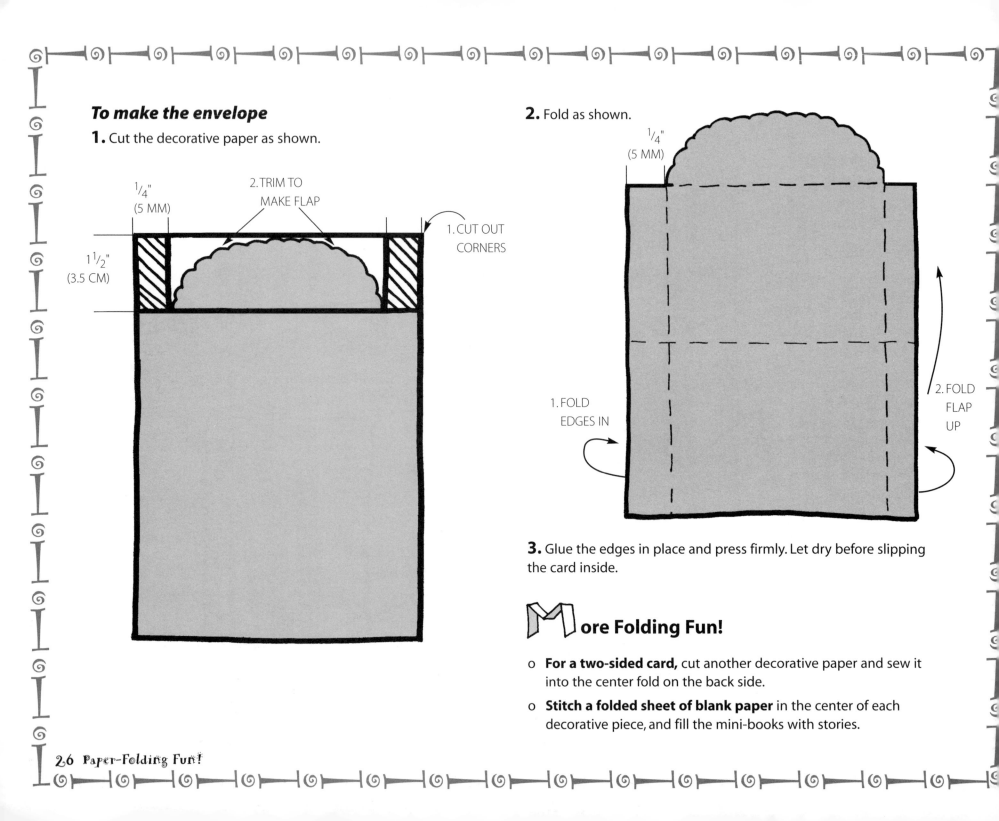

To make the envelope

1. Cut the decorative paper as shown.

2. TRIM TO
MAKE FLAP

1. CUT OUT
CORNERS

¹/₄"
(5 MM)

1¹/₂"
(3.5 CM)

2. Fold as shown.

¹/₄"
(5 MM)

1. FOLD
EDGES IN

2. FOLD
FLAP
UP

3. Glue the edges in place and press firmly. Let dry before slipping the card inside.

More Folding Fun!

o **For a two-sided card,** cut another decorative paper and sew it into the center fold on the back side.

o **Stitch a folded sheet of blank paper** in the center of each decorative piece, and fill the mini-books with stories.

On a Roll!

Here's a new twist on paper crafts! To give a simple piece of paper a whole new dimension, just roll it up to make curls and twists. Use this technique as a quick way to create unforgettable party invites and favors, colorful beads, even a dangling mobile and other cool room decorations. Try your hand at the traditional art of *quilling*, and discover how to create an entire scene out of paper curls. So let's get rolling!

Full-of-Goodies Party Favor

1

Fun to make and even more fun to give! Make these favors "shake, rattle, and roll" by hiding surprise treats and party favors inside! Use decorated paper that matches your party's invitation (see PARTY INVITATION SCROLL, page 30) or use a different paper for each one and let your friends choose their favorite.

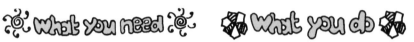

What you need

- Decorative paper, 8½" x 11" (21 x 27.5 cm)
- Toilet-paper tube
- Glue
- Scissors
- Ribbon, 3' (1 m), cut in half
- Filling of your choice: candy, small toys, stickers, a whistle, fun erasers, marbles, a key chain
- Toothpick or nail

What you do

1. Place the decorative paper print side down.

2. Center the cardboard tube on one long edge of the paper and glue the edge to the tube.

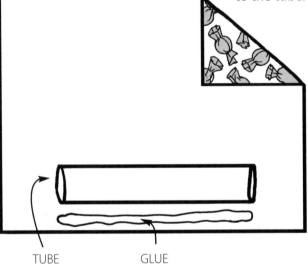

TUBE   GLUE

Roll the paper around the tube; glue the other edge.

3. Cut slits in the paper, stopping about 1" (2.5 cm) from the ends of the tube.

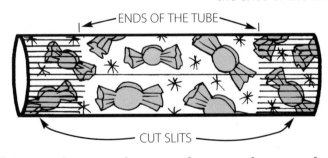

ENDS OF THE TUBE

CUT SLITS

4. Twist the paper at one end just above the tube. Secure the twist with a ribbon bow.

6. Curl (see box) the ends of each strip. Wrap some tight and make other strips a little looser. For variety, curl some strips with the decorative side out and some with the plain side out.

5. Fill the tube. Repeat step 4 to close up the other end.

To curl a paper strip

Wrap the strip tightly around a narrow, straight object like a nail or a toothpick, then remove the object. To make a looser curl, use a pencil.

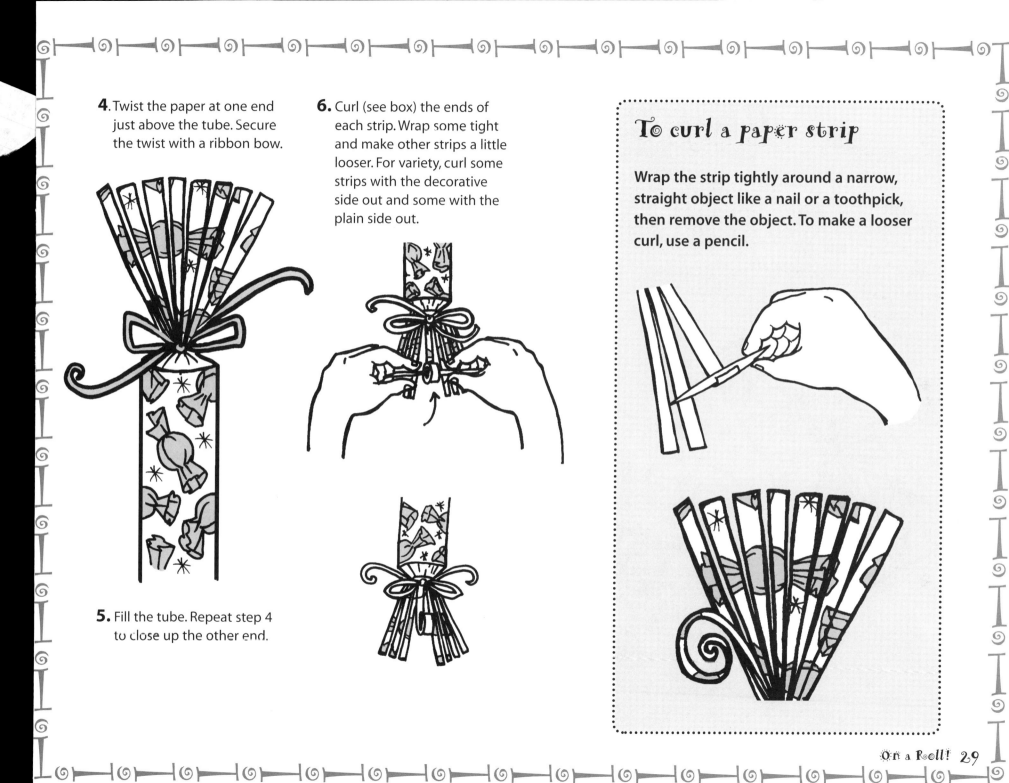

Party Invitation Scroll

In these days of computer-generated party invites, who could resist a hand-lettered scroll? Use decorative paper for your party's theme (like pizzas for a pizza party), then write your own message. Roll the ends toward the center like a scroll, tie with ribbon, and deliver!

What you need

- Scrap paper
- Pencil
- Ruler
- Markers or gel pens
- Solid-color paper, 8½" x 11" (21 x 27.5 cm)
- Waxed paper
- Paintbrush (optional)
- Glue, diluted with a few drops of water, in a shallow dish
- Decorative paper or gift wrap, 8½" x 11" (21 x 27.5 cm)
- Ribbon, 18" (45 cm), two

What you do

1. On scrap paper, write a "rough draft" of your message for your party (don't forget the "Who, What, Where, and When").

2. Using the markers or pens, write your message on the solid-color paper. (To help keep your writing neat, draw lines lightly first with a pencil and ruler.)

3. Cover your work surface with waxed paper (to keep your invitation clean). Place your invitation facedown on the paper.

4. Use the paintbrush or your finger to spread a very thin layer of glue on the back of your invitation, covering it completely. Place the decorative paper, right side up, on top of your glued paper and gently press from the center out in all directions. Let dry completely.

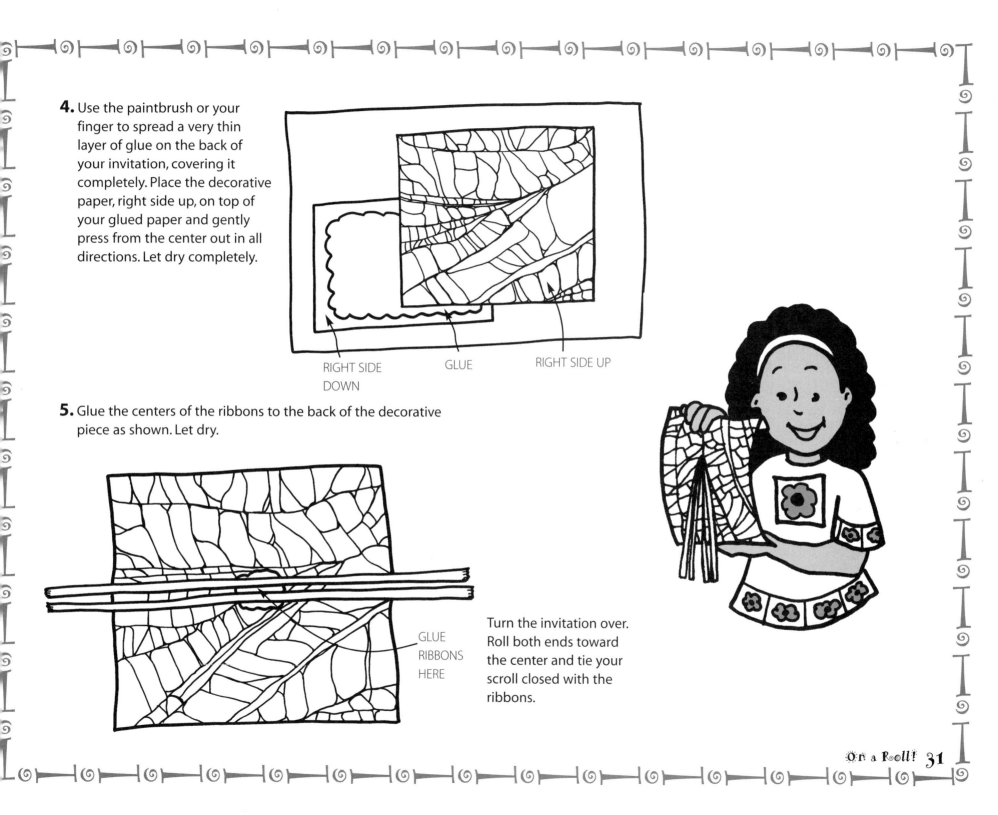

RIGHT SIDE DOWN

GLUE

RIGHT SIDE UP

5. Glue the centers of the ribbons to the back of the decorative piece as shown. Let dry.

GLUE RIBBONS HERE

Turn the invitation over. Roll both ends toward the center and tie your scroll closed with the ribbons.

Glittery Bead Necklace

Ever wish you had a special necklace just the right color to go with that favorite shirt? Paper beads are so easy to make, you can have one in no time! And reflective beads made from foil paper are spectacular!

🌀 What you need 🌀

- Metallic paper
- Ruler
- Pencil
- Scissors
- Toothpick or nail
- Glue
- Needle with a large eye
- Ribbon, decorative cord, or yarn, 24" to 30" (60 to 75 cm)

🎴 What you do 🎴

1. For each bead, cut (page 9) a strip of paper about 2" (5 cm) wide and about 6" (15 cm) long. Draw triangles across the strip as shown. Cut the triangles apart.

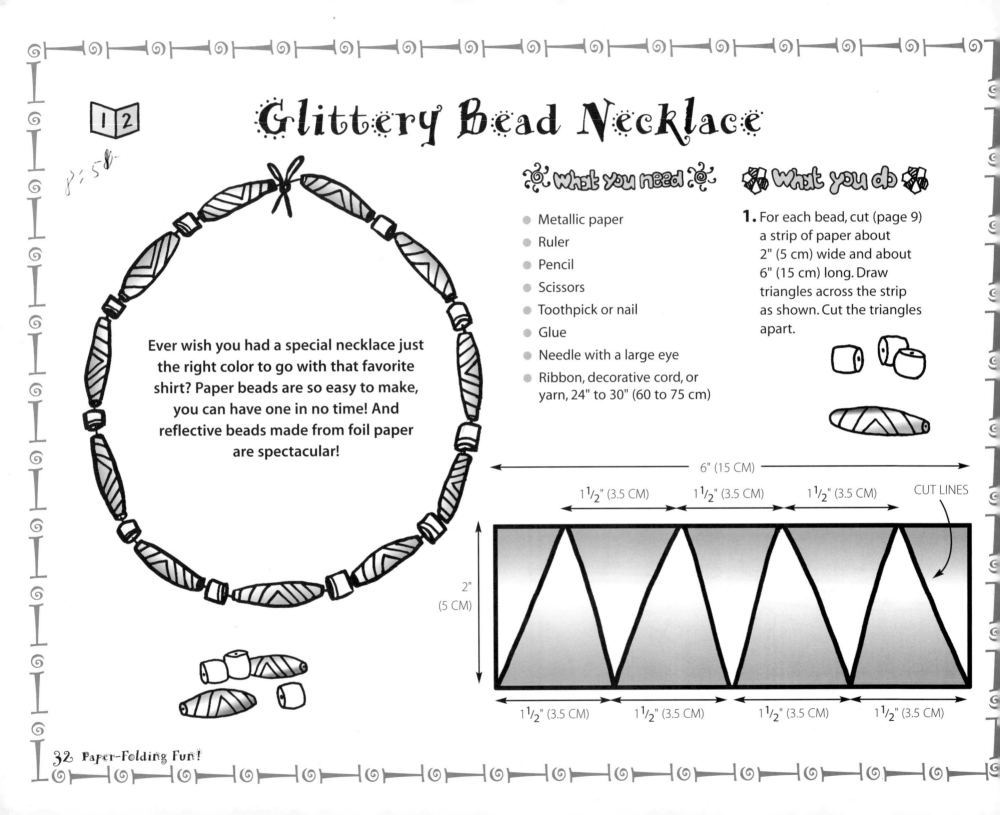

6" (15 CM)

1¹⁄₂" (3.5 CM) 1¹⁄₂" (3.5 CM) 1¹⁄₂" (3.5 CM)

CUT LINES

2" (5 CM)

1¹⁄₂" (3.5 CM) 1¹⁄₂" (3.5 CM) 1¹⁄₂" (3.5 CM) 1¹⁄₂" (3.5 CM)

2. Place the triangle metallic side down. Starting with the wide end, roll it tightly around the toothpick or nail. Glue the tip. When you remove the toothpick, it will leave a hole in the middle of the bead. Roll as many beads as you like.

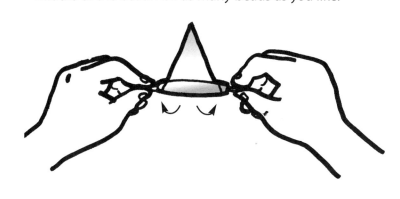

GLUE TIP

HOLE FOR STRING

3. Thread the needle with the ribbon, cord, or yarn and string the beads. Tie the ends of the necklace.

ore Beading Fun!

o **To make different-sized beads**, just change the size of the triangle base. Make *spacers* (narrow beads to string between the larger beads) from $1/4$" x 6" (5 mm x 15 cm) strips.

SPACER   BEAD

o **For chunkier beads**, use a thicker nail or a pencil. Smaller beads may slip inside chunkier beads, however, so it's best to stick with one bead size for each necklace.

o **For a looser, "springier" bead**, remove the nail and let the bead expand slightly before gluing.

o **Roll cutout photos** from old magazines or catalogs for colorful beads with intriguing designs. When the bead is rolled, you won't see the individual pictures, just the colors.

Colorful Quilled Picture

You can create an entire scene by rolling thin strips of paper into loose curls and then gluing them down to make three-dimensional wall art and one-of-a-kind cards. This traditional paper craft, called *quilling*, was very popular in the 1880s and 1890s, and you can still see examples of it in museums. Quilling takes time and patience, but the results are awesome! Save small pieces of paper in your favorite colors from other projects — they are great to use for quilling.

What you need

- Colored pencils
- Card stock, in the dimensions you want the picture to be, or folded in half to use as a card
- Ruler
- Pencil
- Scissors
- Colored paper, in the colors of your sketch
- Toothpick or nail
- Glue, in a shallow dish

What you do

1. With the colored pencils, sketch the outline of your picture on the card stock. A simple scene is best.

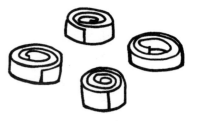

2. Cut the colored paper into 5" (12.5 cm) strips (see box, To Make Quilling Curls). Roll each strip into a curl. Sort the curls by color.

3. Select the area of your picture where you want to start quilling. Dip one flat side of the curl into the glue and position it on your picture.

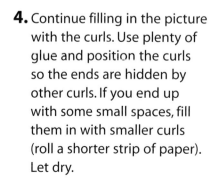

4. Continue filling in the picture with the curls. Use plenty of glue and position the curls so the ends are hidden by other curls. If you end up with some small spaces, fill them in with smaller curls (roll a shorter strip of paper). Let dry.

 To make quilling curls

Cutting the strips

The instructions will indicate how long the strips should be. Mark a piece of paper that length in $\frac{1}{4}$" (5 mm) increments on both ends. You don't have to be too precise; just make them all about the same narrow width.

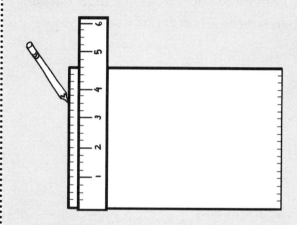

Draw lines across the paper.
Cut along the lines.

Rolling the strips

Roll the strip of paper as tightly as you can around a nail or toothpick.

Place a dot of glue on the end of your curl and press it in place. Remove the nail or toothpick.

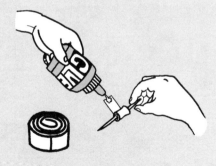

Thin paper creates tight small curls; thicker paper creates a larger, rounder curl. Avoid cardboard; it's too difficult to curl. To create more texture in your picture, vary the width of your strips.

Festive Firecracker

see photograph, back cover

Curl paper into a colorful 3-D display that bursts forth from a cup. Combining related colors looks best — use either warm shades such as red, orange, and yellow, or cool colors like blue, purple, and violet. (For more 3-D creations, see pages 43 to 65.)

what you need

- Glue
- Card stock, three 4" x 8" (10 x 20 cm) strips in bright colors
- Ruler
- Pencil
- Scissors
- Toothpick or nail
- Bright-colored plastic drinking cup
- Scraps of card stock

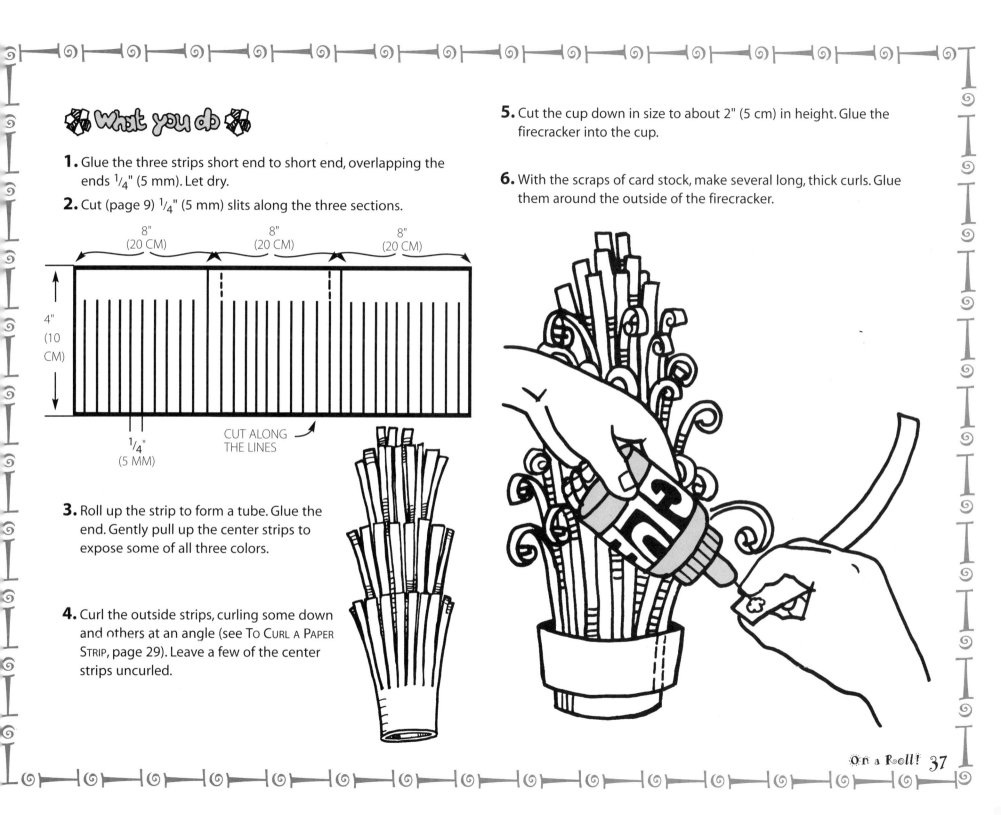

🎆 what you do 🎆

1. Glue the three strips short end to short end, overlapping the ends ¹/₄" (5 mm). Let dry.

2. Cut (page 9) ¹/₄" (5 mm) slits along the three sections.

8"
(20 CM)

8"
(20 CM)

8"
(20 CM)

4"
(10 CM)

¹/₄"
(5 MM)

CUT ALONG THE LINES

3. Roll up the strip to form a tube. Glue the end. Gently pull up the center strips to expose some of all three colors.

4. Curl the outside strips, curling some down and others at an angle (see To Curl a Paper Strip, page 29). Leave a few of the center strips uncurled.

5. Cut the cup down in size to about 2" (5 cm) in height. Glue the firecracker into the cup.

6. With the scraps of card stock, make several long, thick curls. Glue them around the outside of the firecracker.

Quilled Flower Mobile

see photograph, front cover

Here's where your skills in quilling (page 34) will really shine! Create four different quilled flowers and hang them from a mobile where they sway in the breeze.

what you need

- Ruler
- Pencil
- Scissors
- Card stock, in red, green, orange, blue, yellow, and purple
- Toothpick or nail
- Glue
- Sequins
- Gold elastic thread or string
- Metallic twist ties or thin dowels, 8" (20 cm), two

what you do

To cut the strips

1. Cut the following ¹/₄" x 12" (5 mm x 30 cm) strips of card stock: four red, nine green, five orange, three blue, five yellow, three purple (see To MAKE QUILLING CURLS, page 35).

2. Cut three 3" x 9" (7.5 x 22.5 cm) pieces of green card stock.

To make the poinsettia

1. Roll four red strips into quilling curls.

2. Glue two green strips together at one end. Hold the stems in place until dry.

3. Glue the red curls together around the glued end of the green strips as shown.

RED

GREEN

4. About halfway down the stem on either side, fold the ends up. Loosely curl the leaves. Glue the base of the stem.

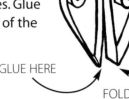

CURL THE LEAVES

GLUE HERE

FOLD HERE

To make the sunflower

1. Roll five orange strips and one blue strip into quilling curls.

2. Loosely curl five yellow strips into oval petals as shown; glue the ends.

3. Fold one green strip in half; glue the three green strips together as shown. Loosely curl the leaves.

GLUE STEMS TOGETHER HERE

AND HERE

4. Glue the orange rolls around the blue one as shown. Slip the stem between the bottom two orange rolls and glue in place.

ORANGE

BLUE CENTER

GLUE STEM BETWEEN TWO ORANGE CURLS

5. Glue on the yellow ovals.

To make the mini-tree

1. Assemble the three pieces of green card stock following steps 1 through 3, FESTIVE FIRECRACKER (page 37). Don't curl the ends of each strip after you pull out the center of the tree.

2. Glue sequins to the ends of both sides of each strip.

To make the lupine

1. Loosely curl three purple and two blue strips to form large petals; glue the ends.

2. Fold two of the green strips in half. Arrange and glue the four green strips as shown. Loosely curl the ends of the two stems.

GLUE TOGETHER HERE

LEAVES   LEAVES

STEMS   STEMS

PURPLE

BLUE   BLUE

PURPLE   PURPLE

3. Glue the purple and blue petals around the stem as shown.

To assemble the mobile

1. Tie a different length of gold thread or string in the center of each flower so they will hang at different heights. For the tree, poke a hole in the tip of one of the strips and tie a length of thread through it.

2. Form an X with the two twist ties, bending one around the other in the center to secure it. If using dowels, tie together with gold thread. Tie a loop of thread in the center for the hanger.

FORM LOOP WITH TWIST TIE

SLIP THREAD THROUGH AND KNOT IT

3. To hang each item, make a small loop in the end of each twist tie and tie on the ornament.

If using dowels, knot the threads around the ends to hang the items.

More Quilling Fun!

You can create all kinds of quilled objects and dangle them from a mobile. Start with a simple sketch of the object, then glue quilled curls into the desired shape, using your sketch as a guide.

o **Make a splash.** Dangle starfish, clam shells, coral, and a tropical fish.

o **Reach for the stars.** How about a solar system mobile with stars, a moon, sun, and planets?

o **Quill up a snowstorm!** Quilled paper makes gorgeous snowflakes. How many different patterns can you create?

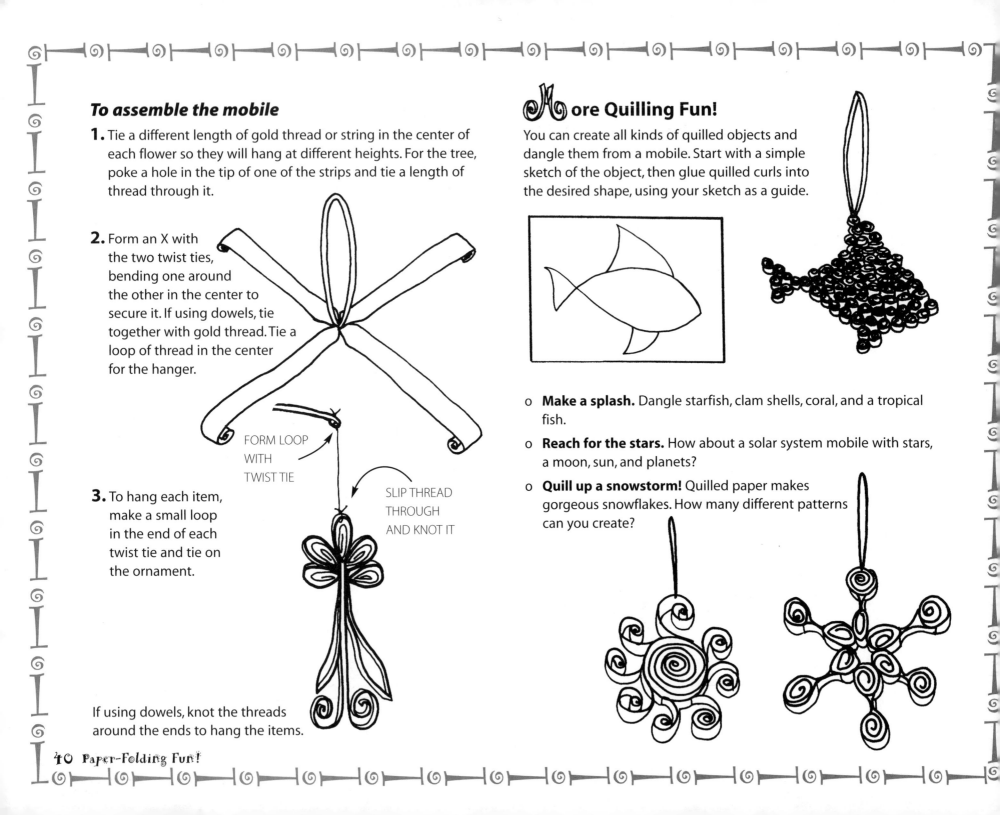

Way-Cool CD Holder

Here's a fun way to store your favorite tunes (it makes a super gift for a music-loving friend, too!). Each shelf is sturdy enough to hold two CDs. Start with four shelves and add more as your collection grows.

Colored corrugated craft cardboard is perfect for this project — it's easy to cut with scissors, but it's sturdy. Let each shelf dry completely before you add the next one.

What you need

- Corrugated craft cardboard: sixteen 1" x 7" (2.5 x 17.5 cm) strips for the columns, five 5" x 8" (12.5 x 20 cm) sections for shelves
- Pencil
- Glue, in a shallow dish
- Small paintbrush
- Book

What you do

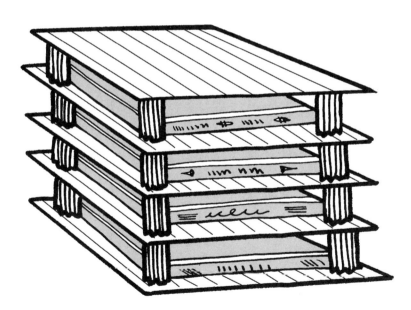

1. Roll each strip around the pencil to form a column; glue the edge.

FACE THE GLUED EDGE INSIDE

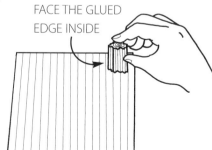

2. Place the first shelf, corrugated side up, on your work surface. Dip one end of a column into the glue and press it onto one corner of the shelf. Face the edge of the roll toward the inside.

Repeat for the other three columns. Before the glue sets, check to be sure that a CD will slide easily into place between the columns; reposition columns if necessary.

3. With the paintbrush, paint the other end of each column heavily with glue. Position another shelf, corrugated side up, directly over the first shelf and press down on all four column supports. Place a book on top of the shelf; let dry completely.

4. Repeat steps 2 and 3 until your last shelf is in place. Make sure your structure remains square by lining up all the columns and squaring each shelf with the previous shelf. Let the glue dry completely before using.

3-D Creations

It's easy to turn a flat sheet of paper into a three-dimensional work of art. All you need are a few special folding and cutting techniques — and lots of imagination! Amaze your friends with pop-up birthday cards, jazz up your room with mobiles and masks, and decorate the table with an awesome centerpiece (but be prepared — the adults who see it may want you to teach *them* how to make it!).

Pop-Up Birthday-Cake Card

1

Are your favorite kinds of greeting cards the ones that jump right out at you when you open them? It's not hard to make a symmetrical pop-up card. When something is *symmetrical*, you can divide it in half and it's exactly the same on both sides. So, fold the card in half, snip a few lines, and presto! — out pops a cake for a very special birthday card. Practice your pop-up on a piece of scrap paper first before trying it with card stock.

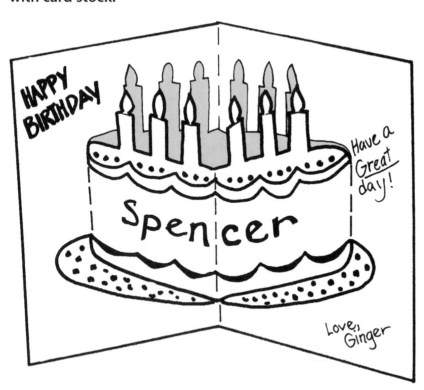

๑ what you need ๑

● Card stock, two 8¹⁄₂" x 11" (21 x 27.5 cm) pieces

● Bone paper folder or Popsicle stick (page 6)

● Pencil

● Scissors

● Glue

● Markers

✿ what you do ✿

1. Fold (page 7) one piece of card stock in half, short edges together.

2. Place the paper with the fold on the right. In the center, starting at the fold line, draw one side of a birthday cake sitting on a plate. Make the cake half no more than 2" (5 cm) wide.

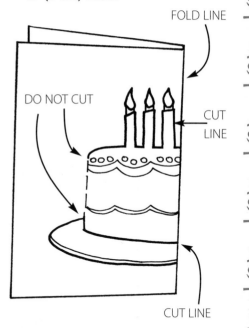

FOLD LINE

DO NOT CUT

CUT LINE

CUT LINE

Remember, you're only drawing half of the cake. If you draw one candle, you'll see two when the card is opened.

3. Cut along the top and bottom of your cake. Don't cut the side, or the cake shape will fall out.

4. Open up your card as shown. Reverse the cake's center crease so it "pops up" from the card.

REVERSE THE CAKE'S CENTER FOLD

5. Close the card with the cake folded forward — this will create fold lines along the sides of the cake. Crease all fold lines.

CLOSE CARD TO CREATE FOLD LINES HERE AND HERE

Spencer

6. Fold the other piece of card stock in half. Lightly glue the back of the piece with the pop-up (but don't glue the pop-up section) and place it inside the folded card. Let dry. Decorate the front and inside of the card.

More 3D Fun!

o **Try these other pop-up ideas.** Be sure to leave a straight section on the side of the shape so you can create fold lines on the sides.

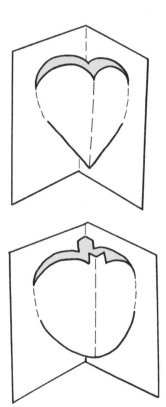

o **Change the size of your card** to create a mini– or gigantic pop-up.

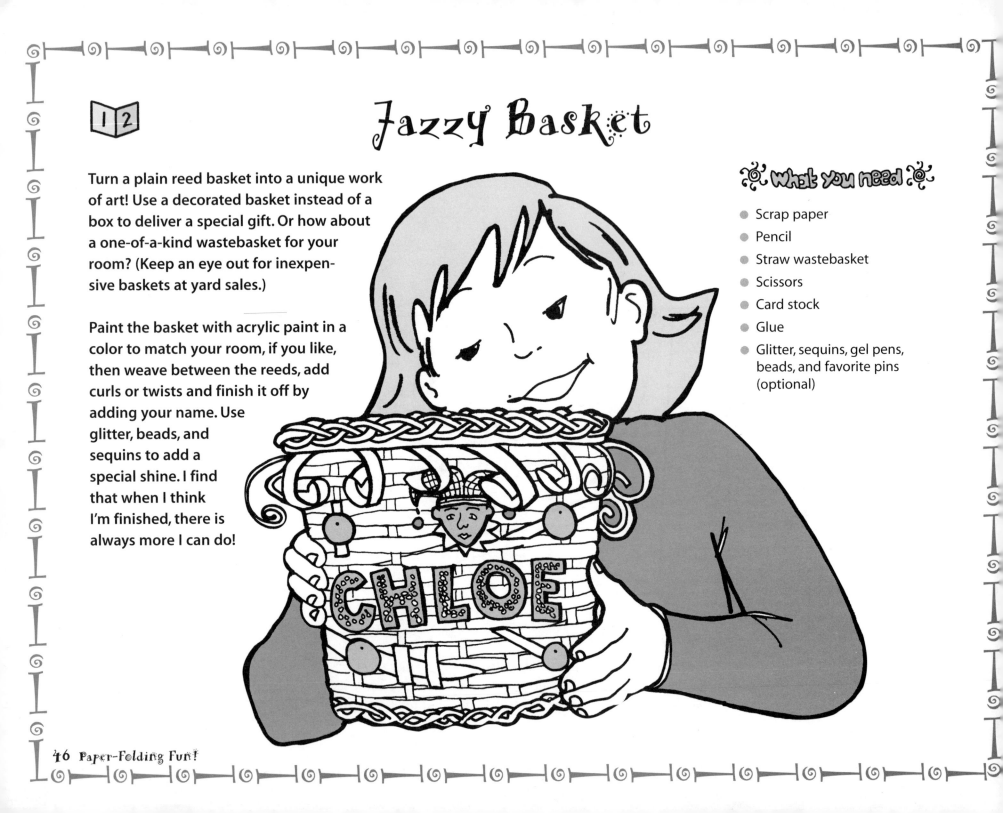

Jazzy Basket

Turn a plain reed basket into a unique work of art! Use a decorated basket instead of a box to deliver a special gift. Or how about a one-of-a-kind wastebasket for your room? (Keep an eye out for inexpensive baskets at yard sales.)

Paint the basket with acrylic paint in a color to match your room, if you like, then weave between the reeds, add curls or twists and finish it off by adding your name. Use glitter, beads, and sequins to add a special shine. I find that when I think I'm finished, there is always more I can do!

What you need

- Scrap paper
- Pencil
- Straw wastebasket
- Scissors
- Card stock
- Glue
- Glitter, sequins, gel pens, beads, and favorite pins (optional)

🌸 What you do 🌸

Create a unique design

Start by sketching the overall design of your basket on scrap paper. What are your favorite colors? Do you want a name on it? Study the illustration of the finished basket for ideas. Are there other paper-folding techniques you've learned in this book that you can use here?

To add a name

1. Cut (page 9) squares of card stock for the letters. I like to use 2" (5 cm) squares for names up to five letters and slightly smaller squares for longer names. Write one letter in each square. Cut out the letters.

2. Cut strips of paper about 1½" (3.5 cm) in length as fasteners for your letters. Each letter needs at least one; some may need two. Glue the fasteners in the center of the back of each letter. Let dry.

GLUE FASTENERS TO BACKS OF LETTERS

3. Slip each fastener between two reeds of the basket and pull it tight. Secure the end by tucking it behind another reed.

INTERIOR OF BASKET

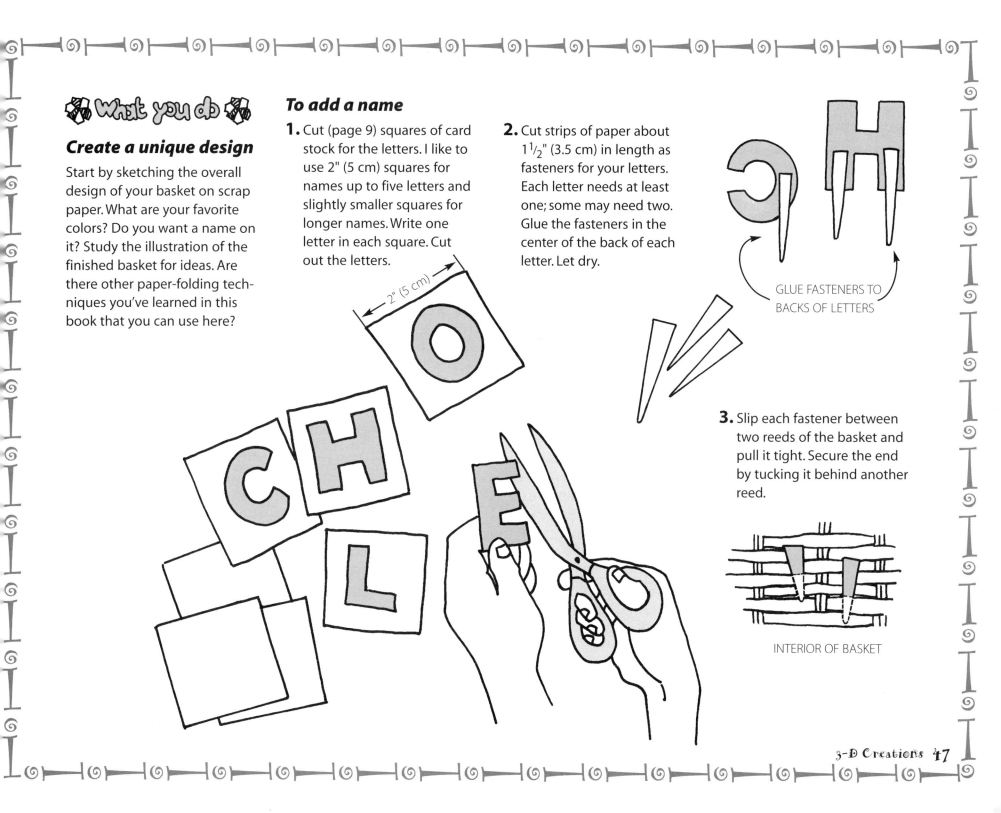

2" (5 cm)

To make other decorations

Cut a supply of long strips of card stock, $1/4$" (5 mm) wide, in a variety of colors. Use them to decorate as desired.

To make diagonal lines: Slip one end of a strip between the reeds near the top of the basket and the other end at the base of the basket several inches (cm) away. Pull the ends tight and secure between reeds.

SECURE ENDS BETWEEN THE REEDS

EXTERIOR OF BASKET

To make vertical lines: Weave strips in and out as shown.

EXTERIOR

INTERIOR

To make curls: Slide a strip between two reeds about 1" (2.5 cm) apart. Center the strip and curl (page 29) both ends around a pencil in opposite directions.

To fold a Jacob's ladder: Glue two strips as shown. Fold them back and forth as shown.

1. FOLD THE VERTICAL STRIP UP

2. FOLD THE HORIZONTAL STRIP TO THE RIGHT

3. FOLD THE VERTICAL STRIP DOWN

4. FOLD THE HORIZONTAL STRIP TO THE LEFT

Repeat this pattern almost all the way to the ends of the strips, leaving enough to tuck them into the reeds and secure on the inside.

Light Switch "Mask"

Turn an ordinary light-switch cover into a face, and turn on your light with the nose! This project is designed to be screwed on over the existing switch-plate cover in your room (ask a parent to help you remove the screws safely and attach your mask). Make a fearsome mask to scare your friends — or how about several faces for different moods?

What you need

- *Template-making supplies:* tracing paper, pencil, ruler, scissors, stiff paper or light-weight cardboard
- Craft knife (page 6)
- Old newspapers or piece of thick cardboard
- Card stock, $8\frac{1}{2}$" x 11" (21 x 27.5 cm)
- Decorative papers in assorted colors and textures, for the face features
- Glue
- Toothpick, nail, or knitting needle

What you do

To make the template

Trace the SWITCH PLATE template (page 120) onto the tracing paper. Cut it out, marking all openings.

Trace the tracing-paper template onto the stiff paper or cardboard. Transfer all markings. Cut out the template. Use the craft knife to cut out holes for the screws and the rectangle for the light switch.

To make the mask

1. Center the cardboard template on the background paper. Trace all openings. Cut out the circles and rectangle. Cut rounded corners on the background paper; cut a wavy edge if you like.

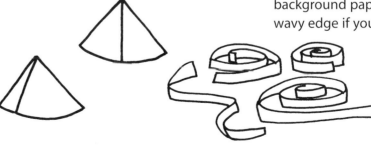

2. Make a 1" (2.5 cm) cut in the four rounded corners. Overlap at the slits and glue. This will raise the mask slightly so it fits over your existing switch plate.

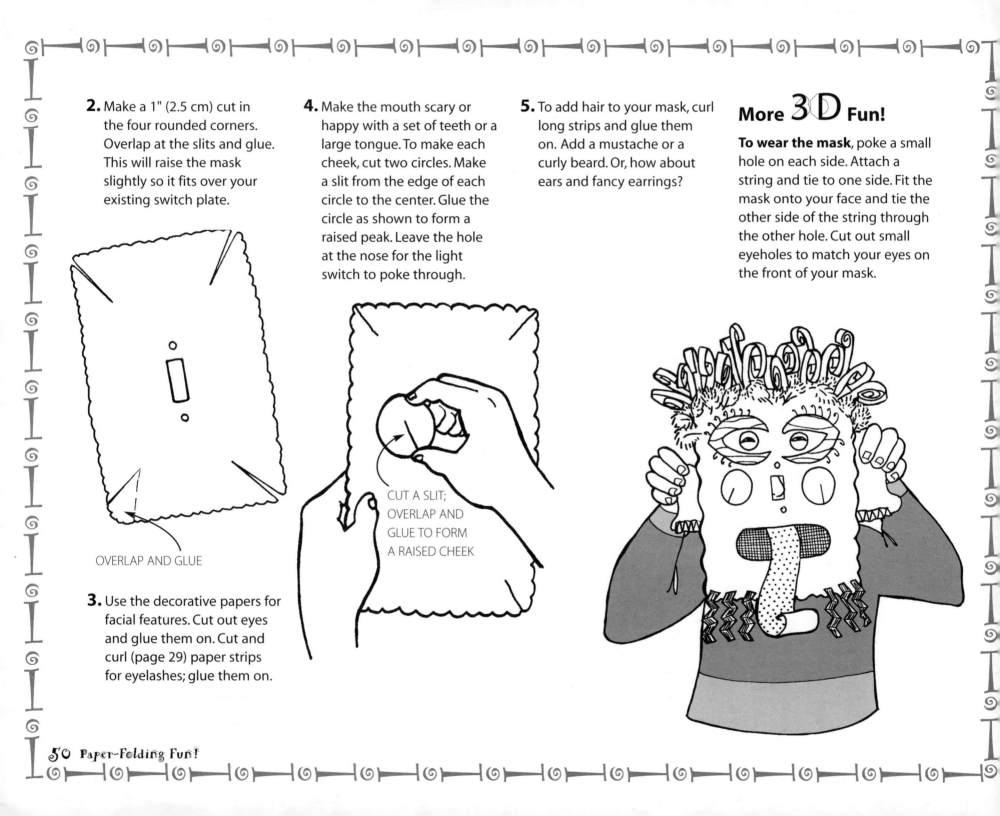

OVERLAP AND GLUE

3. Use the decorative papers for facial features. Cut out eyes and glue them on. Cut and curl (page 29) paper strips for eyelashes; glue them on.

4. Make the mouth scary or happy with a set of teeth or a large tongue. To make each cheek, cut two circles. Make a slit from the edge of each circle to the center. Glue the circle as shown to form a raised peak. Leave the hole at the nose for the light switch to poke through.

CUT A SLIT; OVERLAP AND GLUE TO FORM A RAISED CHEEK

5. To add hair to your mask, curl long strips and glue them on. Add a mustache or a curly beard. Or, how about ears and fancy earrings?

More 3D Fun!

To wear the mask, poke a small hole on each side. Attach a string and tie to one side. Fit the mask onto your face and tie the other side of the string through the other hole. Cut out small eyeholes to match your eyes on the front of your mask.

see photograph of spiral star (page 53), front cover

Geometric Mobile

These 3-D shapes each start with a flat piece of paper. Just draw some lines, cut, and fold. Then, dangle one from another and let them spin and twirl! Add a spiral star (page 53) if you like!

what you need

- *Template-making supplies:* tracing paper, pencil, ruler, scissors, stiff paper or lightweight cardboard
- Card stock: three 6" (15 cm) squares; one 5" (12.5 cm) square
- Craft knife (page 6)
- Old newspapers or a piece of thick cardboard
- Glue
- Glitter glue, gel pens, sequins, and other decorations
- Toothpick
- Gold thread

what you do

To make the templates

Trace the OVAL and CIRCLE templates (page 118) onto tracing paper, marking only the outside lines and the X marks. Cut out the templates on the outsides lines only.

Trace the tracing-paper templates onto the stiff paper or cardboard. Transfer the X marks. Cut out on the outside lines.

To make the mobile

1. Trace the cardboard templates onto two of the 6" (15 cm) card-stock squares. Cut out the shapes and draw the curving lines as shown on the templates on page 118.

2. Place one of the other 6" (15 cm) card-stock squares on the newspapers. With the ruler, draw a faint X from the opposite corners. These lines will serve as the reference point for all other lines.

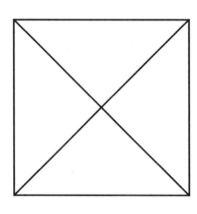

3. On one half of the square, draw right-angle lines beginning and ending at the diagonal line as shown. Make the lines about 1/2" (1 cm) apart.

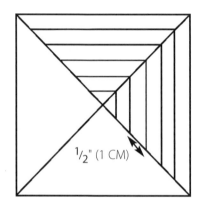

1/2" (1 CM)

4. Fill the other side of the square with right-angle lines. Make these lines start and end *between* the other lines you drew.

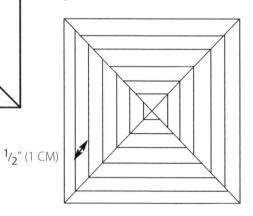

1/2" (1 CM)

5. Use the craft knife and the ruler to cut on the right-angle lines, forming a series of triangles. *Don't* cut on the diagonal lines.

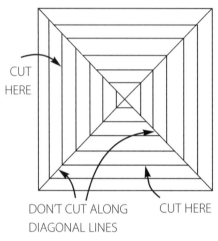

CUT HERE

DON'T CUT ALONG DIAGONAL LINES

CUT HERE

6. Decorate both sides of the paper. Let the glue dry.

7. Beginning on one side, fold every other cut triangle forward on the diagonal line. Fold back every other strip on the opposite side.

8. Follow steps 2 through 8 for the 5" (12.5 cm) square. Follow steps 5 through 8 for the circle and the oval.

9. Use the toothpick to poke a hole at the top of each shape. Use lengths of gold thread to connect the shapes and to hang the mobile.

More 3D Fun!
Make a spiral star

Jazz up your mobile by dangling this out-of-this-galaxy star at the bottom!

1. Cut a 6" (15 cm) square of card stock. Cut squares out of each corner as shown. Cut it to have jagged edges like a star.

1¹/₂" (3.5 CM)

1¹/₂" (3.5 CM)

1¹/₂" (3.5 CM)

2. Cut a multi-sided shape in a contrasting color to fit in the center; glue in place.

3. On a 3" (7.5 cm) square of paper, draw a spiral as shown.

Cut along the line. Glue the outer edge of the spiral to the circle so the spiral pops up.

4. Curl (page 29) very thin strips of paper and glue them to the back of the star. Poke a hole in one of the star points. Hang with thread from your mobile.

Circle-of-Hearts Centerpiece

Display this decoration as a freestanding panel on a mantel, or arrange it as a four-sided centerpiece (fasten the edges with a paper clip) — and check out the intricate star formation when you view it from the top! You'll amaze everyone, because this project looks more difficult to make than it really is. When the celebration is over, just flatten your project like an accordion and store it until next time.

What you need

- *Template-making supplies:* Tracing paper, pencil, scissors, stiff paper or lightweight cardboard
- White and decorative paper for the hearts
- Bone paper folder or Popsicle stick (page 6)
- Pink card stock, three 12" x 18" (30 x 45 cm) pieces
- Ruler
- Glue
- Paper clip (optional)

What you do

To make the template

Trace the HEART 1 AND HEART 2 templates (page 117) onto the tracing paper. Cut them out.

Trace the tracing-paper templates onto the stiff paper or cardboard. Cut them out.

To make the hearts

1. Trace the HEART 1 cardboard template four times on the white paper; cut out the hearts. Trace HEART 2 cardboard template four times on patterned paper; cut out the hearts. Glue a patterned heart in the center of each white heart.

2. Fold (page 7) each heart in half, with the decorative side facing out. Open the fold.

To make the panels

1. Fold (page 7) one piece of pink card stock in ha1f, long edges together. Open the fold. Cut along the fold line. Glue the two pieces end to end to make one 6" x 36" (15 x 90 cm) piece. Repeat with the other two pieces of pink card stock.

2. With one piece of pink card stock (panel 1), make an eight-panel accordion (page 12).

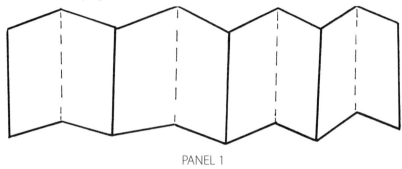

PANEL 1

3. Cut (page 9) $2^3/_4$" (7 cm) off the short end of the second piece of card stock (panel 2). Score (page 8) a $3/_8$" (1 cm) tab on each end and fold to the back. Now fold the panel into eight accordion sections, as in step 2. Open the folds.

FOLD $3/_8$" (1 CM) TABS TO THE BACK BEFORE FOLDING INTO AN ACCORDION

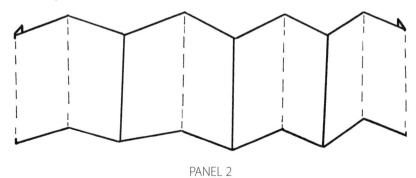

PANEL 2

4. On the back fold lines of panel 2, tear or cut an opening, centered about $1^1/_4$" (3 cm) in from the edges.

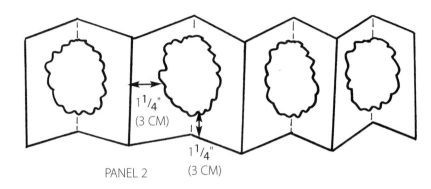

$1^1/_4$" (3 CM)

$1^1/_4$" (3 CM)

PANEL 2

5. Cut 4" (10 cm) off the short end of the last piece of card stock (panel 3). Score a $1/_2$" (1 cm) tab on both short ends of the panel and fold the tabs to the back. Now fold the panel into eight accordion sections, as in step 2.

FOLD $1/_2$" (1 CM) TABS TO THE BACK BEFORE FOLDING INTO AN ACCORDION

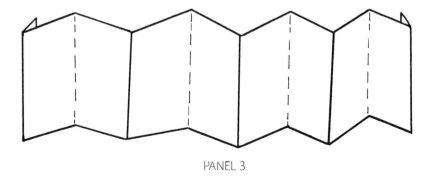

PANEL 3

6. Repeat step 4 to create openings in panel 3, making them slightly larger than the ones in panel 2.

To assemble the centerpiece

1. Stand the three panels as shown, with the longest in the back and the shortest (the one with the largest openings) in the front.

PANEL 1

PANEL 2

PANEL 3

2. To connect panels 1 and 2, glue along the tabs on the back of panel 2 and along each front fold line. Place panel 2 over panel 1, securing the tabs first and then gluing fold to fold.

3. To attach panel 3, glue the tabs and press the panel in place over the other two panels.

Fold the panels into an accordion and lay it flat to dry.

2. GLUE TABS OF PANEL 3 TO BACK OF PANEL 2

1. GLUE TABS OF PANEL 2 TO BACK OF PANEL 1

PANEL 3

PANEL 2

PANEL 1

4. Open your centerpiece. Glue the outside edges of a white heart to panel 1, in the center of the first opening.

LINE UP THE CENTER FOLDS ON THE PANEL AND THE HEART

GLUE TO INSIDE BACK PANEL HERE AND HERE

Line up the heart's fold line with the fold lines of the panels, so that the heart pops out through a cut window when the centerpiece is open, and then folds in half when the centerpiece is folded up.

Repeat with the other three hearts.

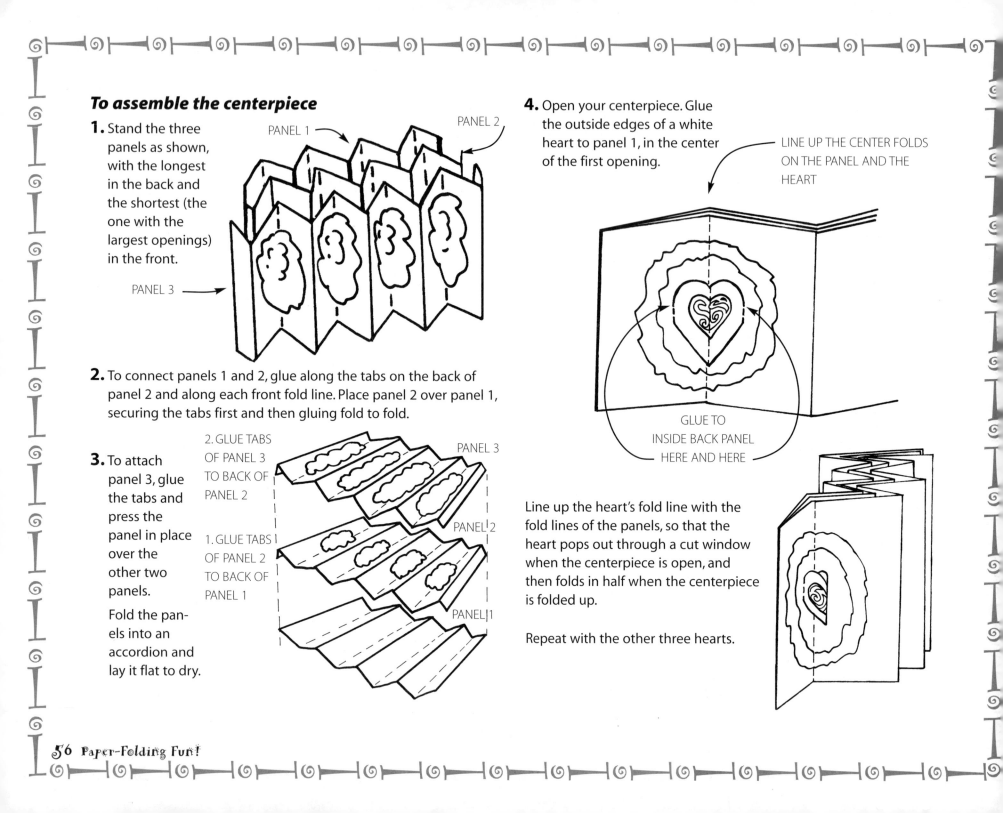

Friendly Dragon

see photograph, front cover

You'll be a very popular baby-sitter when you bring along the supplies for this creature! It sways back and forth, swishing its brightly colored tail, thanks to an unusual folding technique and an uneven gluing pattern. Fold it flat into a small square, and then let it pounce! Play with it like a Slinky, or have fun arranging it someplace so it will take someone by surprise.

✤ What you need ✤

- Decorative paper, 4" (10 cm) squares in two contrasting patterns, six each
- Bone paper folder or Popsicle stick (page 6)
- Glue
- Card stock: 1½" x 6" (3.5 x 15 cm) of pink for the mouth; ¾" x 3" (2 x 7.5 cm) of red for the tongue; scraps in contrasting colors for the feet and tail
- Scissors
- Wiggly eyes

✤ What you do ✤

To make the dragon's body

1. In this step, always fold the right sides of the paper together. Fold (page 7) a square in half. Open the fold. Refold in the other direction. Open the fold. Fold corner to corner, and open the fold. Your square should look like this:

2. Turn the square over. Push down on the center fold, so the center point points down.

Continue to bring the two diagonal fold lines together, and flatten the shape into a perfect square one-fourth the size of the original square.

Repeat with the remaining squares.

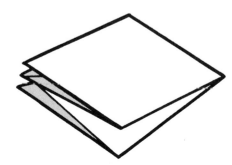

3. To form the body, glue the squares together, alternating the decorative papers, following this pattern: Glue the first two squares together with folded point to folded point.

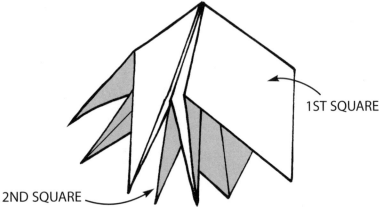

1ST SQUARE

2ND SQUARE

4. Rotate the third square one-half turn to the *right* (so the square opens out to the side instead of up and down). Glue to the second square.

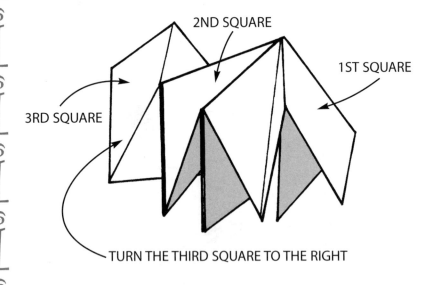

2ND SQUARE

1ST SQUARE

3RD SQUARE

TURN THE THIRD SQUARE TO THE RIGHT

5. Glue on the fourth square, again matching folded point to folded point.

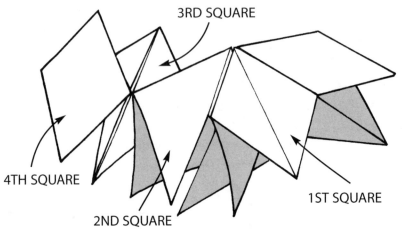

3RD SQUARE

4TH SQUARE

1ST SQUARE

2ND SQUARE

6. Rotate the fifth square one-half turn to the *left* and glue it on.

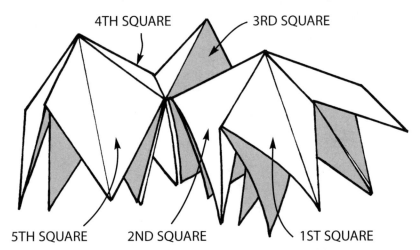

4TH SQUARE

3RD SQUARE

5TH SQUARE

2ND SQUARE

1ST SQUARE

Repeat this pattern, gluing the next square folded point to folded point. Glue on the last two squares folded point to folded point. Stretch out the dragon and let it dry completely.

7. For the mouth, fold the strip of pink paper in half. Round the corners on one end.

FOLD LINE

CUT LINE

8. Cut out four feet and glue each one to the underside of a square section. Cut out several zigzag strips in bright colors for a tail and glue them to the last square. Glue on wiggly eyes.

FOOT

TAIL

Open the fold and glue to the top of the first square on the inside.

Fold the red strip for the tongue back and forth like an accordion and glue in the mouth.

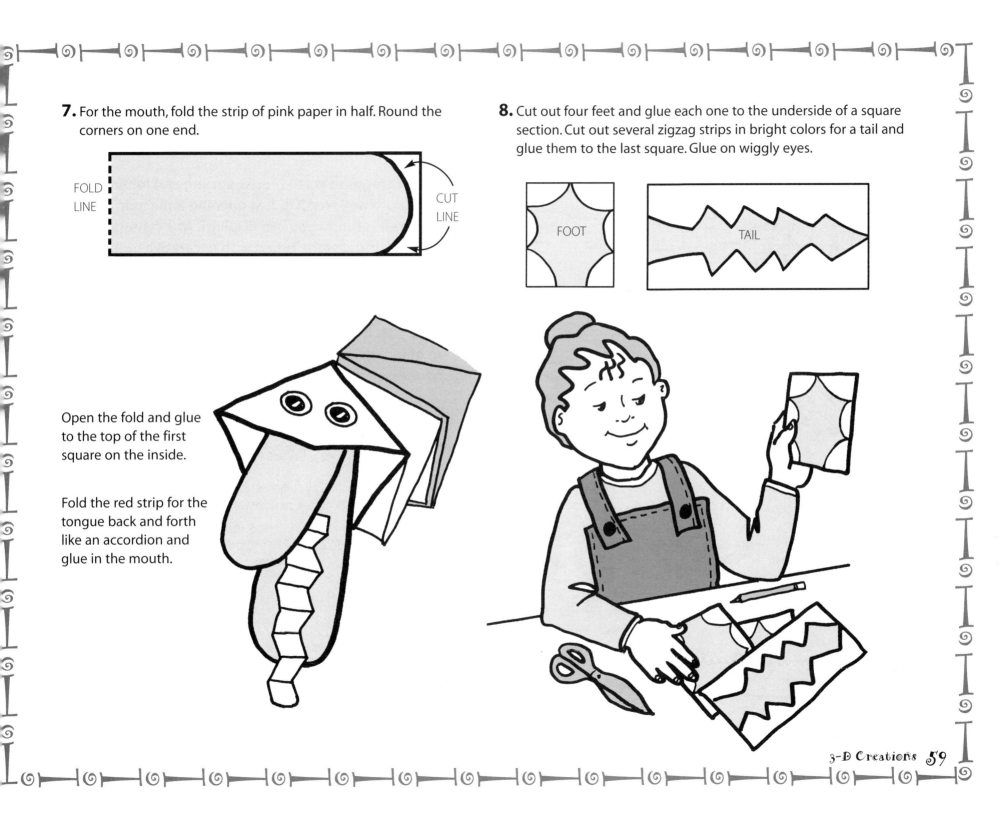

Flying "Fish"

see photograph, back cover

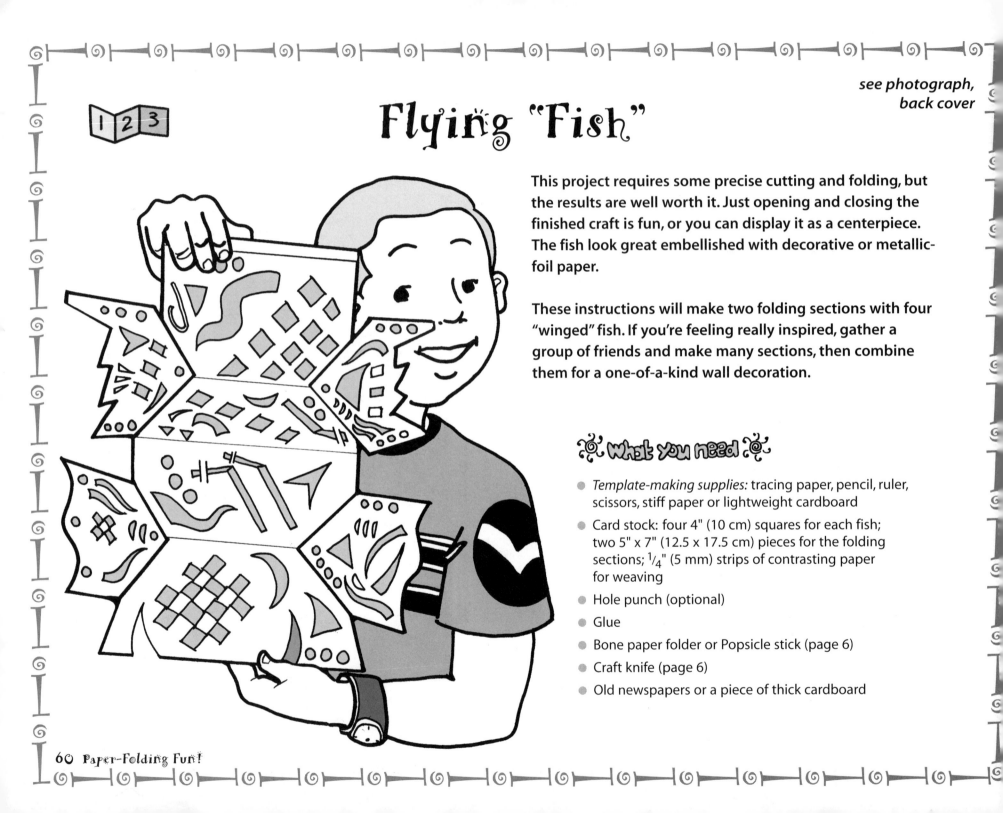

This project requires some precise cutting and folding, but the results are well worth it. Just opening and closing the finished craft is fun, or you can display it as a centerpiece. The fish look great embellished with decorative or metallic-foil paper.

These instructions will make two folding sections with four "winged" fish. If you're feeling really inspired, gather a group of friends and make many sections, then combine them for a one-of-a-kind wall decoration.

What you need

- *Template-making supplies:* tracing paper, pencil, ruler, scissors, stiff paper or lightweight cardboard
- Card stock: four 4" (10 cm) squares for each fish; two 5" x 7" (12.5 x 17.5 cm) pieces for the folding sections; 1/4" (5 mm) strips of contrasting paper for weaving
- Hole punch (optional)
- Glue
- Bone paper folder or Popsicle stick (page 6)
- Craft knife (page 6)
- Old newspapers or a piece of thick cardboard

To make the template

Trace the FISH template (page 117) onto tracing paper and cut it out.

Trace the tracing-paper template onto the stiff paper or cardboard. Cut it out.

To make the fish

1. Trace the cardboard template onto each card-stock square and cut out four fish, two of each color.

2. Use the craft knife to cut a series of slits and weave the narrow strips of paper in and out. Cut and punch out small designs. Use the cutout shapes in contrasting colors to decorate each fish.

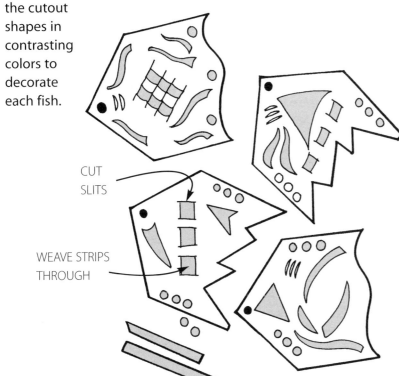

CUT SLITS

WEAVE STRIPS THROUGH

To make the folding sections

1. On a 5" x 7" (12.5 x 17.5 cm) card stock, score (page 8) a line $^3/_8$" (1 cm) in on one of the short edges. Fold (page 7) this tab to the back. Repeat with the other card-stock section.

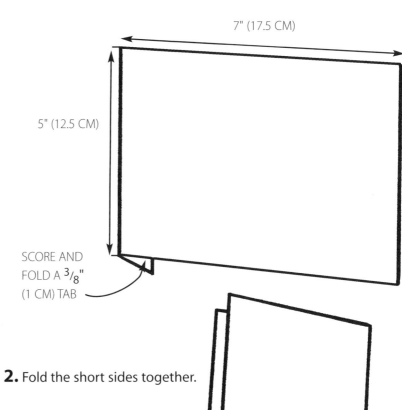

7" (17.5 CM)

5" (12.5 CM)

SCORE AND FOLD A $^3/_8$" (1 CM) TAB

2. Fold the short sides together.

3. Mark dots on the folded section and sides as shown.

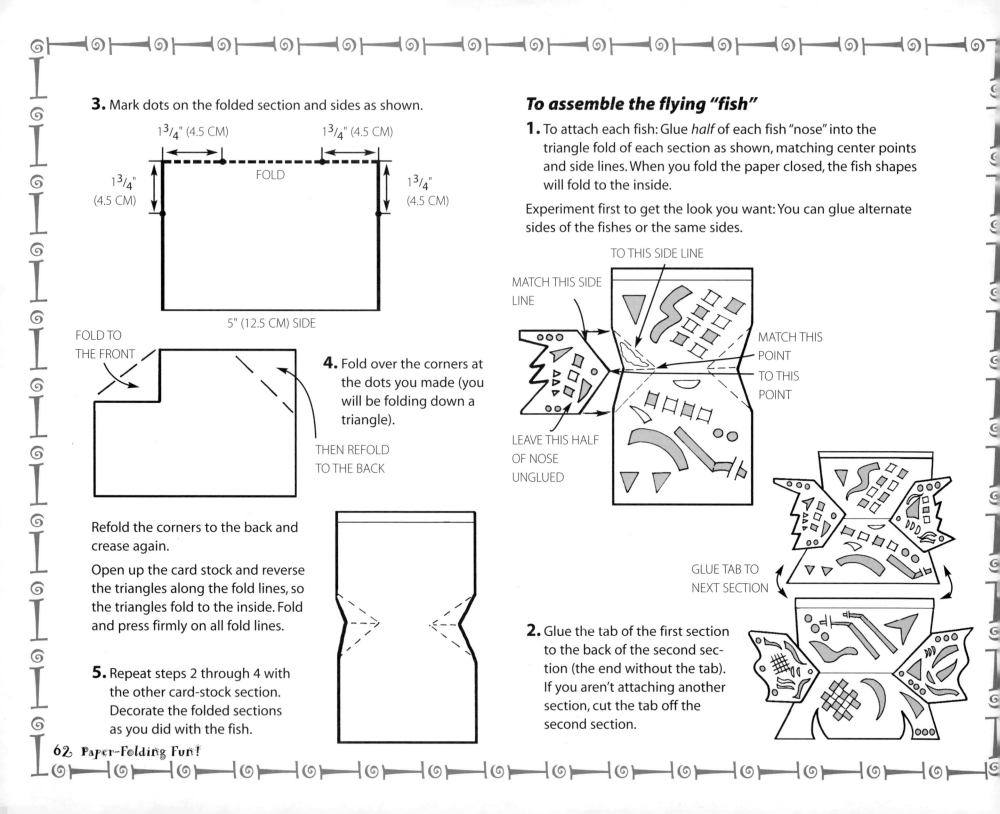

1³/₄" (4.5 CM)   1³/₄" (4.5 CM)

FOLD

1³/₄"
(4.5 CM)

1³/₄"
(4.5 CM)

5" (12.5 CM) SIDE

FOLD TO
THE FRONT

4. Fold over the corners at the dots you made (you will be folding down a triangle).

THEN REFOLD
TO THE BACK

Refold the corners to the back and crease again.

Open up the card stock and reverse the triangles along the fold lines, so the triangles fold to the inside. Fold and press firmly on all fold lines.

5. Repeat steps 2 through 4 with the other card-stock section. Decorate the folded sections as you did with the fish.

To assemble the flying "fish"

1. To attach each fish: Glue *half* of each fish "nose" into the triangle fold of each section as shown, matching center points and side lines. When you fold the paper closed, the fish shapes will fold to the inside.

Experiment first to get the look you want: You can glue alternate sides of the fishes or the same sides.

TO THIS SIDE LINE

MATCH THIS SIDE
LINE

MATCH THIS
POINT
TO THIS
POINT

LEAVE THIS HALF
OF NOSE
UNGLUED

GLUE TAB TO
NEXT SECTION

2. Glue the tab of the first section to the back of the second section (the end without the tab). If you aren't attaching another section, cut the tab off the second section.

interlocking Origami Beads

These beads are an example of *origami*, a traditional Japanese art of paper folding that you may already be familiar with. (For another, brand-new style of origami, see pages 80 to 83). These beads are a little challenging, but it's really cool the way the two halves interlock, holding together without any glue.

Make several and hang them as individual holiday ornaments. Or gather a group of friends to make lots of beads, then string them together into a festive garland for a holiday tree or doorway.

what you need

- Card stock, origami, decorative or metallic paper: 2³/₄" (7 cm) squares in contrasting colors, two per bead
- Popsicle stick or bone paper folder (page 6)
- Pencil

what you do

1. In this step, it's important to always fold the right sides of the paper together. If you're working with paper that's the same color on both sides, choose one to be the "right" side.

Fold (page 7) a square diagonally; open the fold. Fold diagonally the other way; open the fold. Fold in half; open the fold. Fold in half the other way; open the fold.

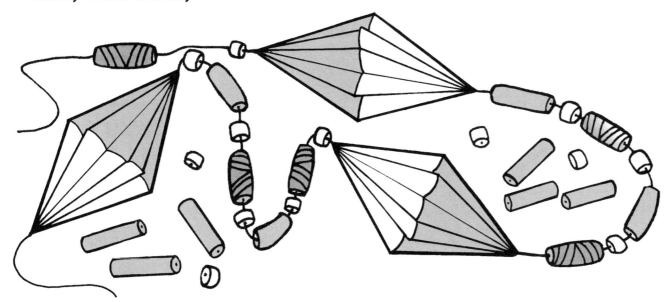

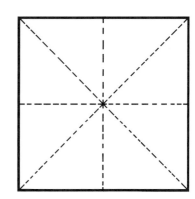

2. Flip the paper over so the center point points down. Bring two opposite diagonal fold lines together in the center as shown.

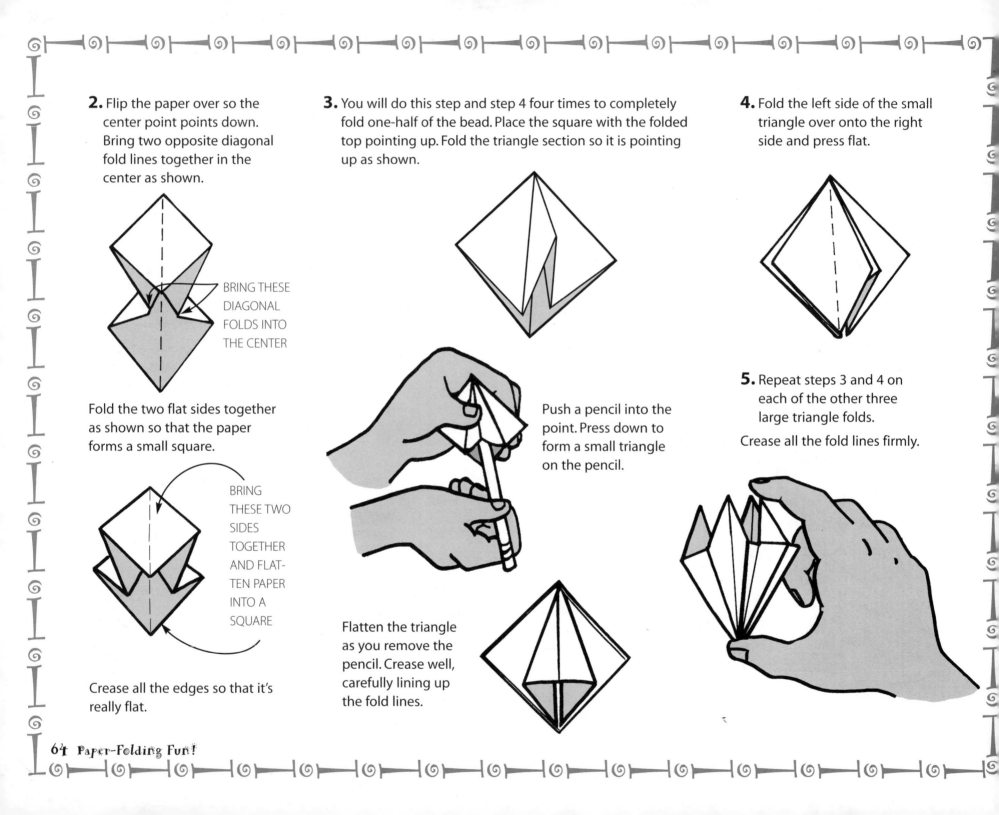

BRING THESE DIAGONAL FOLDS INTO THE CENTER

Fold the two flat sides together as shown so that the paper forms a small square.

BRING THESE TWO SIDES TOGETHER AND FLATTEN PAPER INTO A SQUARE

Crease all the edges so that it's really flat.

3. You will do this step and step 4 four times to completely fold one-half of the bead. Place the square with the folded top pointing up. Fold the triangle section so it is pointing up as shown.

Push a pencil into the point. Press down to form a small triangle on the pencil.

Flatten the triangle as you remove the pencil. Crease well, carefully lining up the fold lines.

4. Fold the left side of the small triangle over onto the right side and press flat.

5. Repeat steps 3 and 4 on each of the other three large triangle folds.

Crease all the fold lines firmly.

6. Repeat steps 1 through 5 with the other paper square.

7. Sliding the bead halves together is a little tricky and takes patience. Place the two halves, A and B, on a flat surface. Slide point A of the left half into fold B of the right half.

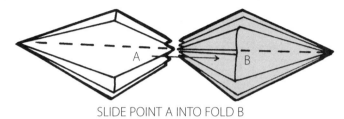

SLIDE POINT A INTO FOLD B

Flip to the next section and slide point B into fold A.

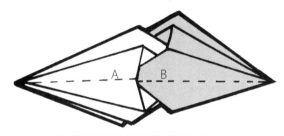

SLIDE POINT B INTO FOLD A

8. Continue working your way around, sliding the points into the folds.

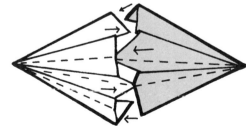

You may find that a point has ended up in the wrong fold — just gently pull it out (without pulling out any of the properly positioned points) and slip it into the proper one.

Take your time, working on one point at a time. Congratulations! You have just made an origami bead!

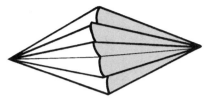

Finishing Touches

✳ **TO MAKE A GARLAND, use a large needle or the end of a paper clip to poke a hole in the ends of each bead. Slip one end of a length of metallic thread or embroidery floss into the hole (apply a little glue to the end of the thread to stiffen it first, if necessary) and add a bit of glue to the end of the bead to hold it in place. Glue the other end. String rolled paper bead spacers (pages 32 to 33) between the origami beads if you like.**

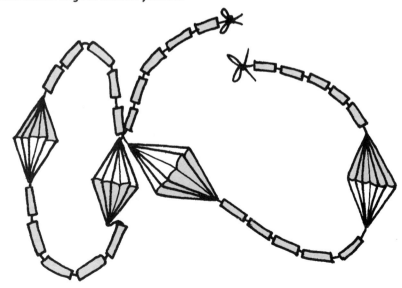

Magical Folds

Dazzle your friends with "seems like magic" paper-folding tricks like surprise pop-ups, secret messages, even a tiny book that opens into an amazing 3-D star. The special folds and cuts aren't difficult but they give you surprising results — when you know the secrets behind them.

Surprise Photo Memory Folder

Celebrate time spent with a favorite relative or a special friend. The folder has a secret pop-up message, a pocket for a little card, plus a spot for a photo, perfect for preserving a memory.

✺ what you need ✺

- Ruler
- Pencil
- Bone paper folder or Popsicle stick (page 6)
- Card stock: 5½" x 18" (13.5 x 45 cm) for the folder; 3" x 5" (7.5 x 12.5 cm) in a contrasting color for the pocket
- Markers and gel pens
- Photo, trimmed to 4" x 5" (10 x 12.5 cm)
- Glue
- Paper: 5½" (13.5 cm) square for the pop-up message; 3" x 11" (7.5 x 27.5 cm) in a contrasting color for the card

🌸 What you do 🌸

To make the folder

1. Measure and score (page 8) four lines on the card stock as shown.

2. Fold (page 7) the sides in on the scored lines as shown. There will be a small gap between the two edges when they are folded in place. Fold the short side over again. Decorate the outside of the folder.

3. Open all the folds. Glue the photo at the top of the middle panel. Write the date and the event under the picture.

SCORE   SCORE   SCORE

$5^7/_8$" (14.5 CM)

6" (15 CM)   6" (15 CM)

$2^{15}/_{16}$" (7.5 CM)

FOLD   FOLD

SHORT SIDE   LONG SIDE

Photo Memories

FOLD AGAIN

Spencer's 2nd Birthday
November 1999

To make the pop-up

1. On the paper square, write your memories of the event.

2. Fold the paper in half so the message is on the outside. Open the fold.

3. Turn the square over. Fold it diagonally. Open the fold. Fold it diagonally the other way. Open the fold.

4. Refold the square, bringing the top and bottom center fold lines together to form two triangles.

5. Place the pop-up into the left panel of the folder, lining up the point of the pop-up with the center of the left-hand fold. Be sure the pop-up will open properly when you open the folder before you glue it in place.

6. Glue the outside of the right triangle and press it in place.

Now glue the outside of the left triangle. Refold the folder to press the triangle in place. Let dry.

To make the pocket

Glue the pocket onto the right panel as shown.

GLUE BOTTOM AND SIDES

To make the card

Fold the card paper into a four-panel accordion (page 12). Decorate the card and place it in the pocket.

ore Folding Fun!

o **Present the folder** to the recipient in a handmade box (see FLAT BOX WITH LID, page 109). Use your memory folder to record an annual event, like baking holiday cookies with Grandma, and add a new folder to the box each year!

o **Ask each friend** to bring a favorite photo to your next sleepover. You provide the supplies — and everyone makes a photo folder to take home!

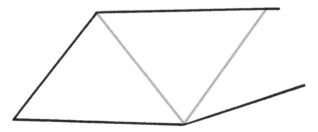

Mystery Triangle

This is a quick project with amazing results. From a strip of paper you create a book that folds flat into a triangle, dangles as a multi-sided room decoration, or folds into a standing pyramid. Be prepared to teach your friends — they'll all want to know the secret!

On the dangling book sections:

My Trip to Camp.

Day 1 my bunk mates.

Day 2 took a swim test.

Day Hit C

Day 11 At horseback riding the horse rolled on my lunch!

Day 10 wrote home and got two Letters

Day 9 Learned a new camp song.

Day 8 Chloe and Jane are my best friends!

What you need

- *Template-making supplies:* tracing paper, pencil, ruler, scissors, stiff paper or lightweight cardboard
- Card stock, 3½" x 18" (8.5 x 45 cm)
- Bone paper folder or Popsicle stick (page 6)

What you do

To make the template

Trace the TRIANGLE template (page 117) onto the tracing paper. Cut it out. Trace the tracing-paper template onto the stiff paper or cardboard. Cut it out.

Finishing Touches

To make the folded triangle

1. Trace the cardboard template onto the card stock as shown. Cut off the end pieces.

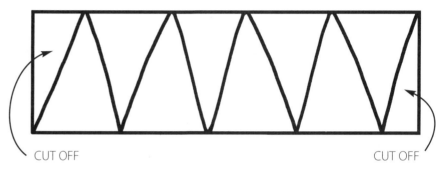

CUT OFF   CUT OFF

2. Score (page 8) all the lines.

3. Fold (page 7) on the scored lines accordion-style, back and forth, into a triangle. Match edges carefully as you fold.

✳ **WRITE IN EACH TRIANGULAR SECTION**, using both sides. You'll have 16 sections in all. Use it as a journal — perfect for recording your favorite memories of two weeks at camp, for example. Or how about riddles on one side and the answers on the other? Then refold into a triangle.

✳ **DECORATE EACH SECTION** with glitter, sequins, or beads and hang in your room.

Mystery Message Circle

If you liked making the MYSTERY TRIANGLE (page 69), you'll love this little circle! With some fancy folding techniques, you can turn a long strip of paper into an accordion spiral with a secret message inside. Hang it on a cord for a wearable greeting. Make one with a secret message inside for a friend.

What you need

- Bone paper folder or Popsicle stick (page 6)
- Card stock: 1³/₄" x 12" (4.5 x 30 cm) for the circle; ¹/₂" x 5¹/₂" (1 cm x 13.5 cm) in a contrasting color for the band
- Ruler
- Markers
- Needle or pin
- Scissors
- Decorative cording, 30" (75 cm)

What you do

To make the circle

1. With the longer strip of card stock, make an eight-panel accordion (page 12).

2. Unfold the strip. Score (page 8) each rectangle diagonally as shown.

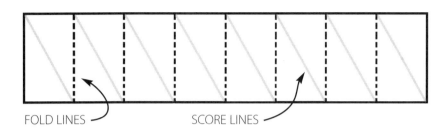

FOLD LINES ⟍   SCORE LINES ⟍

3. Begining at one end, fold back and forth on the scored lines and the accordion folds. You will be folding triangles that spiral around each other into a circle.

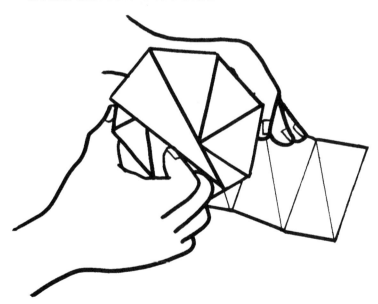

4. Unfold the strip and write your secret message. Refold.

To make the band

1. Wrap the remaining piece of paper around the circle (it will overlap). With the needle or pin, poke through both ends of the band in the center.

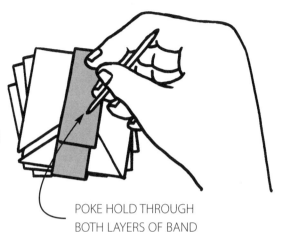

POKE HOLD THROUGH
BOTH LAYERS OF BAND

2. Slip the band off the circle. Cut up to the hole on one end and down to the hole on the other end.

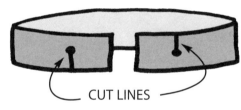

CUT LINES

3. Wrap the band around the folded circle and slip one slit into the other to lock the band in place.

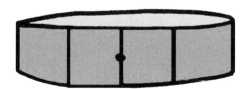

4. Slide the cording through the paper band, and knot the ends.

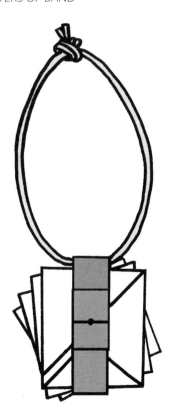

Circular Star Memory Book

see photograph, front cover

See if you can stump your friends with this folding star!

I recommend practicing with lightweight paper first.

Bring the two covers together and you have a 3-D multi-pointed star that you can hang or arrange several different ways on a table. Open it flat on a desk like a Slinky, or place the opened covers flat against a wall for a different effect.

What you need

- Bone paper folder or Popsicle stick (page 6)
- Card stock: five 6" (15 cm) squares; two $3\frac{1}{8}$" (8 cm) squares for the covers
- Glue

What you do

To fold the squares

1. In this step, always fold the right sides of the paper together. Fold (page 7) one square in half, top to bottom. Open the fold and fold the square side to side. Open the fold. Flip the paper over, and fold diagonally. Open the fold.

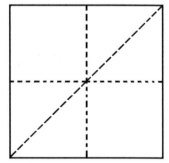

2. Turn the square over. Push down on the center fold, so the center point points down.

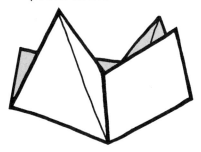

Continue to bring the two diagonal fold lines together, and flatten the shape into a perfect square one-fourth the size of the original square.

3. Repeat steps 1 and 2 for the other squares. Be sure your squares are folded exactly and all fold lines are pressed very flat.

To assemble the journal

1. Place one square with the folded tip at the top. Glue on a second square, matching folded tips.

2. Repeat step 1 until all the squares are glued on.

3. Open the book, making sure the pages stick to each other only where you placed the glue. Leave open to dry.

4. Center the folded squares on the bottom cover and glue it in place. Repeat with the top cover.

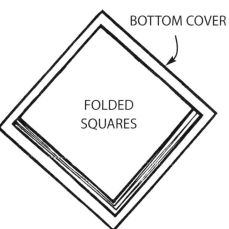

BOTTOM COVER

FOLDED SQUARES

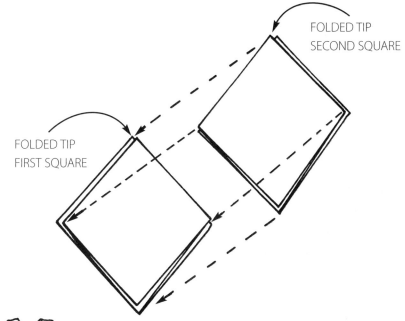

FOLDED TIP SECOND SQUARE

FOLDED TIP FIRST SQUARE

More Folding Fun!

o **Use decorative papers** and write on the blank sides.

o **Use a different color** for each square.

o **For holiday ornaments**, make 3" (7.5 cm) squares out of holiday gift wrap. Decorate with glitter and sequins. Fold into stars and hang in windows or as ornaments.

o **Use more than five pages** for your book and see what happens!

Finishing Touches

✳ **TO HANG, open the book and place the covers together, forming a star. Poke a small hole through the tops of the covers. Thread monofilament through the hole and knot it.**

Colorful Star Journal

see photograph, back cover

This is my favorite paper-folding trick! It's the same folding technique used in the CIRCULAR STAR MEMORY BOOK (page 72), but the assembly is different. I like to create a pattern with squares of three bold colors. You can use the squares as a journal, making the book as long as you like, or just display the pattern on a table, letting it rest on its "points." Or, hang it from one end with monofilament and let it twist and turn. The squares can be any size as long as they are all exactly the same.

what you need

- Card stock: seven or more 6" (15 cm) squares in the colors or patterns of your choice; two $3\frac{1}{8}$" (8 cm) squares for the covers
- Bone paper folder or Popsicle stick (page 6)
- Glue
- Decorations for the front cover
- Markers and gel pens (optional)

✿ What you do ✿

1. With the 6" (15 cm) squares, follow the steps for *To fold the squares,* Circular Star Memory Book (page 72).

2. Place one square so the folded tip is at the top. Glue on a second square, with its folded tip at the bottom.

SECOND SQUARE

FOLDED TIP
GLUE HERE

FOLDED TIP

FIRST SQUARE

3. Repeat step 2 until all the squares have been glued on.

4. Gently open the journal completely and let it dry. (If the book dries all folded up, you may find that it won't open completely.)

5. Refold the journal. Glue the covers to the top and bottom squares. Once dry, decorate the cover of your book. Open the book and write or decorate the inside, if you want.

More Folding Fun!

o **Use white paper.** Decorate one side of each paper with pastels or watercolors. Write your message on the blank side.

o **Create a decorative border** around each message with markers, stickers, or stamps.

o **Gather your friends together** and teach everyone this fancy fold. Then, glue the pages together and have each friend decorate or write a message on a square to create an unforgettable memory book for a friend in the hospital or one who is moving away!

Color Magic Flip-Flop

Just opening and closing this book is fun! It's only strips of paper and a simple accordion fold, but the effect is amazing! I love to make this book with neon-colored pages and black for the covers and the folded section. Flip the pages like a traditional book or extend it to its full length. My students once created a book 18' (5.5 m) long using this form!

This is my favorite style for a memory book (use each narrow strip to record a memory).

What you need

- Card stock: two 5$\frac{1}{4}$" x 12" (13 x 30 cm) pieces for the covers and the accordion; twenty-one 1$\frac{1}{2}$" x 5$\frac{1}{2}$" (3.5 x 13.5 cm) strips in assorted colors

- Bone paper folder or Popsicle stick (page 6)

- Glue

- Markers or pens (optional)

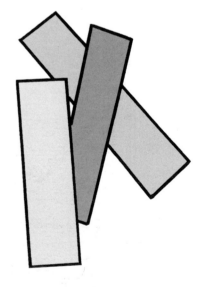

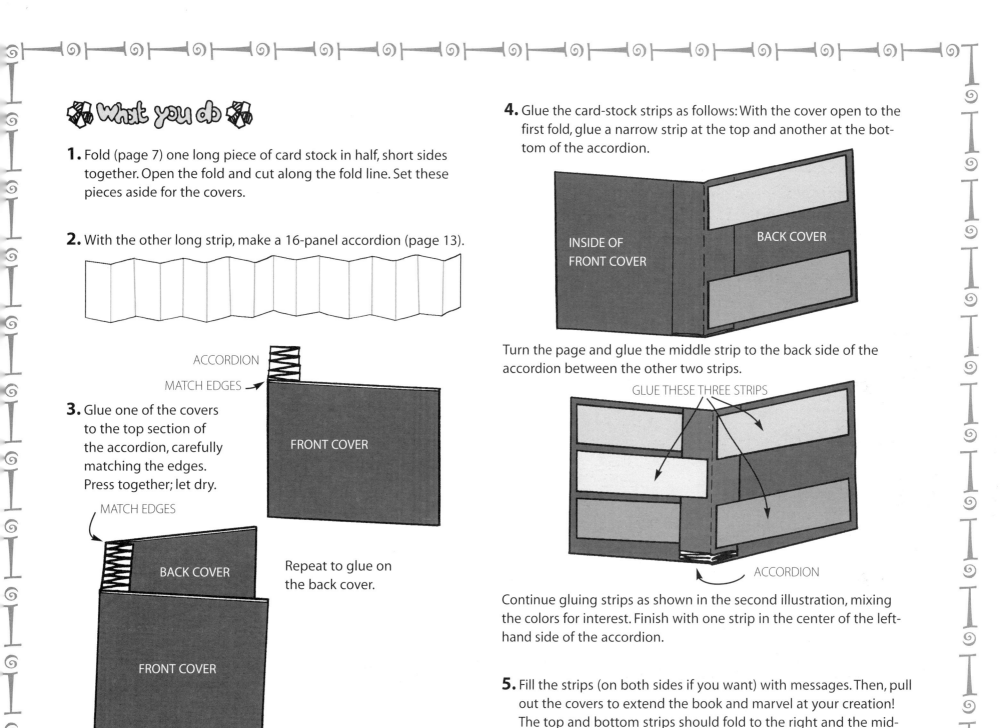

✶ what you do ✶

1. Fold (page 7) one long piece of card stock in half, short sides together. Open the fold and cut along the fold line. Set these pieces aside for the covers.

2. With the other long strip, make a 16-panel accordion (page 13).

3. Glue one of the covers to the top section of the accordion, carefully matching the edges. Press together; let dry.

ACCORDION

MATCH EDGES →

FRONT COVER

MATCH EDGES

BACK COVER

FRONT COVER

Repeat to glue on the back cover.

4. Glue the card-stock strips as follows: With the cover open to the first fold, glue a narrow strip at the top and another at the bottom of the accordion.

INSIDE OF FRONT COVER

BACK COVER

Turn the page and glue the middle strip to the back side of the accordion between the other two strips.

GLUE THESE THREE STRIPS

ACCORDION

Continue gluing strips as shown in the second illustration, mixing the colors for interest. Finish with one strip in the center of the left-hand side of the accordion.

5. Fill the strips (on both sides if you want) with messages. Then, pull out the covers to extend the book and marvel at your creation! The top and bottom strips should fold to the right and the middle strips should fold to the left.

ore Folding Fun!

Make a slipcase

Slip your book into this open-ended pocket for safekeeping.

1. Cut (page 9) a 5¹/₂" x 13¹/₂" (13.5 x 33.5 cm) piece of card stock. Score (page 8) lines as shown.

2. Fold on the scored lines. Fold slipcase around the book and glue the tab in place. The top and bottom will be open so you can slip the book in and out.

¹/₂" (1 CM)

¹/₂" (1 CM)

TAB

6¹/₄" (15.5 CM)

6¹/₄" (15.5 CM)

TAB

SCORE LINES

Finishing Touches

✷ **DECORATE YOUR COVER. Gel pens look great on a black cover.**

✷ **TO MAKE ADDITIONAL PAGES, cut another 12" (30 cm) strip and fold into another 16-panel accordion (see page 13). Before attaching the cover, glue the first fold of the second accordion to the last fold of the first accordion. Cut additional narrow strip pages.**

Kaleidoscope Origami

Chances are you're already familiar with *origami*, the Japanese art of folding paper into intricate designs and clever animals. Here's a whole new style called kaleidoscope origami. It's also known as "tea-bag folding," because it originated in Holland where tea bags are sold in beautiful decorative papers that are used for this craft. Use these intricate paper pinwheels for ornaments, book-cover and card decorations, and more!

Experimenting with different patterns of paper is half of the fun of making these. Try alternating two solid colors or two decorative papers. Metallic papers also make awesome kaleidoscopes that shimmer in the light.

(To make origami beads, see pages 63 to 65.)

Circle-of-Squares Kaleidoscope

What you need

- Card stock, or metallic or decorative paper, eight 2" (5 cm) squares
- Glue
- Bone paper folder or Popsicle stick (page 6)

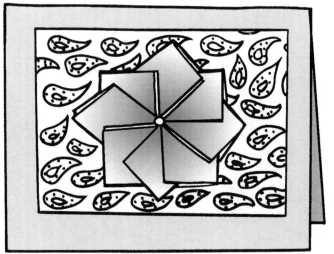

🌸 What you do 🌸

1. Fold (page 7) a square in half (if using paper with a pattern or color on one side only, fold with wrong sides together). Then fold it in half again.

2. Repeat with the other seven squares of paper.

3. Put a dab of glue on the back of the folded point of one of the squares and slide it into another square at an angle. The folded point of the square should point into the center of the kaleidoscope.

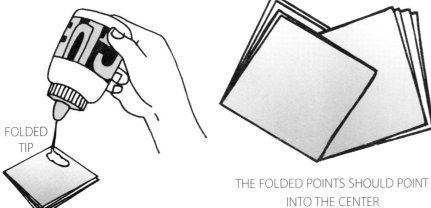

FOLDED TIP

THE FOLDED POINTS SHOULD POINT INTO THE CENTER

4. Repeat with the remaining squares to form the kaleidoscope. All the folded points of the squares should point to the center of the kaleidoscope. Glue the squares together on the back of the kaleidoscope to hold them in place. To make a set of note cards, see page 83.

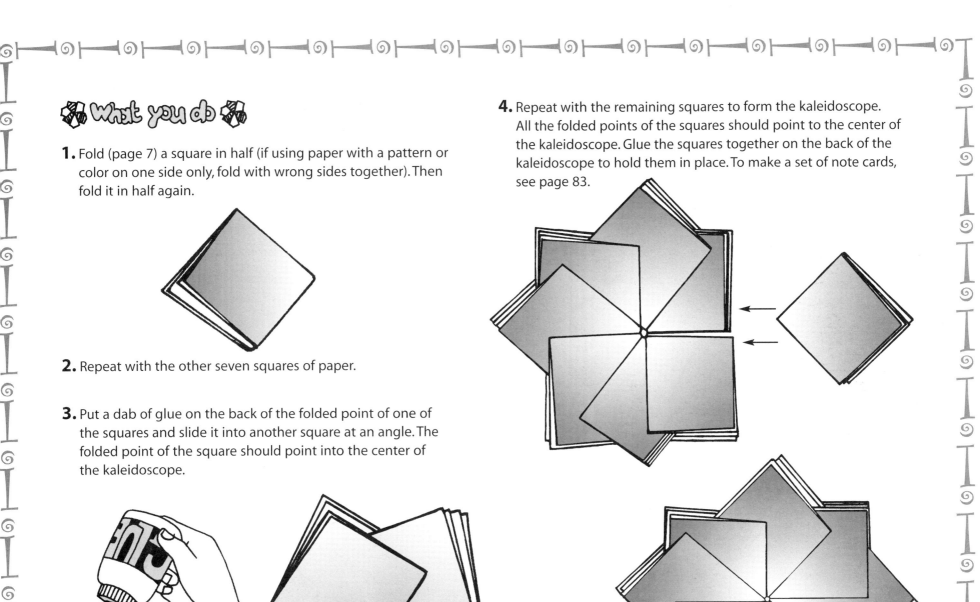

Center-Star Kaleidoscope

see photograph, front cover

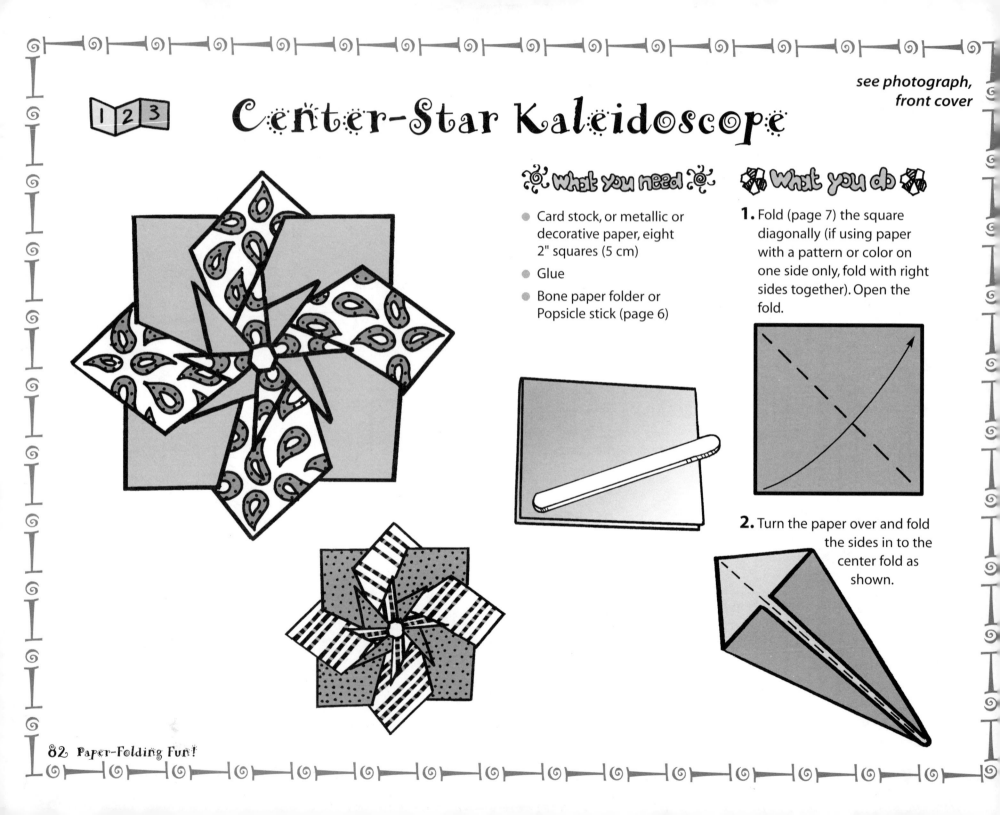

❁ What you need ❁

- Card stock, or metallic or decorative paper, eight 2" squares (5 cm)
- Glue
- Bone paper folder or Popsicle stick (page 6)

❁ What you do ❁

1. Fold (page 7) the square diagonally (if using paper with a pattern or color on one side only, fold with right sides together). Open the fold.

2. Turn the paper over and fold the sides in to the center fold as shown.

3. Turn the paper over. Fold the bottom point up as shown.

4. Repeat steps 1 through 3 with the other seven squares of paper.

5. To interlock the pieces, put a dab of glue along the left edge on the back side of one piece and slip it between the fold lines of another piece as shown. The next one will slip into the fold lines of the one you just glued in place.

INSERT GLUED EDGE OF
SECOND SQUARE IN HERE

6. Continue around, forming a circle, until you have attached all eight. You'll see the points of a star forming, and there will be a small hole in the center. Before the glue sets, adjust your finished kaleidoscope if necessary.

More Folding Fun!

Make a set of note cards. Fold four pieces of 6" x 9" (15 x 22.5 cm) card stock in half and glue a kaleidoscope origami in the center of each one. Decorate the cards with glitter, gel pens, or markers, if you like.

Now, deliver them in a handmade box (see FLAT BOX WITH LID, page 109) and decorate the lid with a kaleidoscope, too!

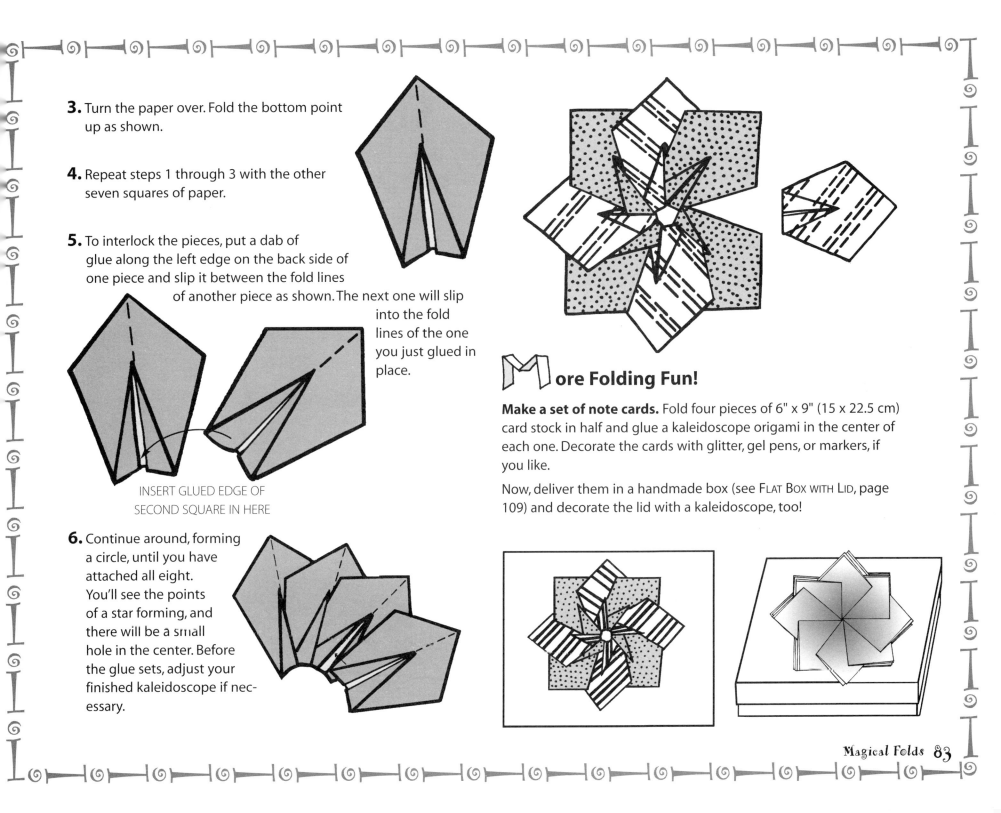

Weave it!

You probably have lots of interesting or beautiful items woven out of cloth — but did you know you can weave with paper, too? The basic technique is easy, and choosing the colors to create the pattern is part of the fun. You can incorporate old calendars and magazine photos into your weaving, create a heart-shaped basket or a handy camping mat, jazz up the covers of your textbooks, even weave a favorite melody into a colorful wall hanging.

Weaving is Easy!

Once you've got the hang of the basic weaving technique (and that won't take long!), you're ready for any of the projects in this chapter.

When you weave with paper, you weave thin strips horizontally (the *weft*) in and out of a background piece of paper with vertical lines cut in it (the *warp*).

To mark and cut the warp lines
The instructions for the specific craft you're making will tell you how wide to make these lines and what size margin to leave at the edges of the paper.

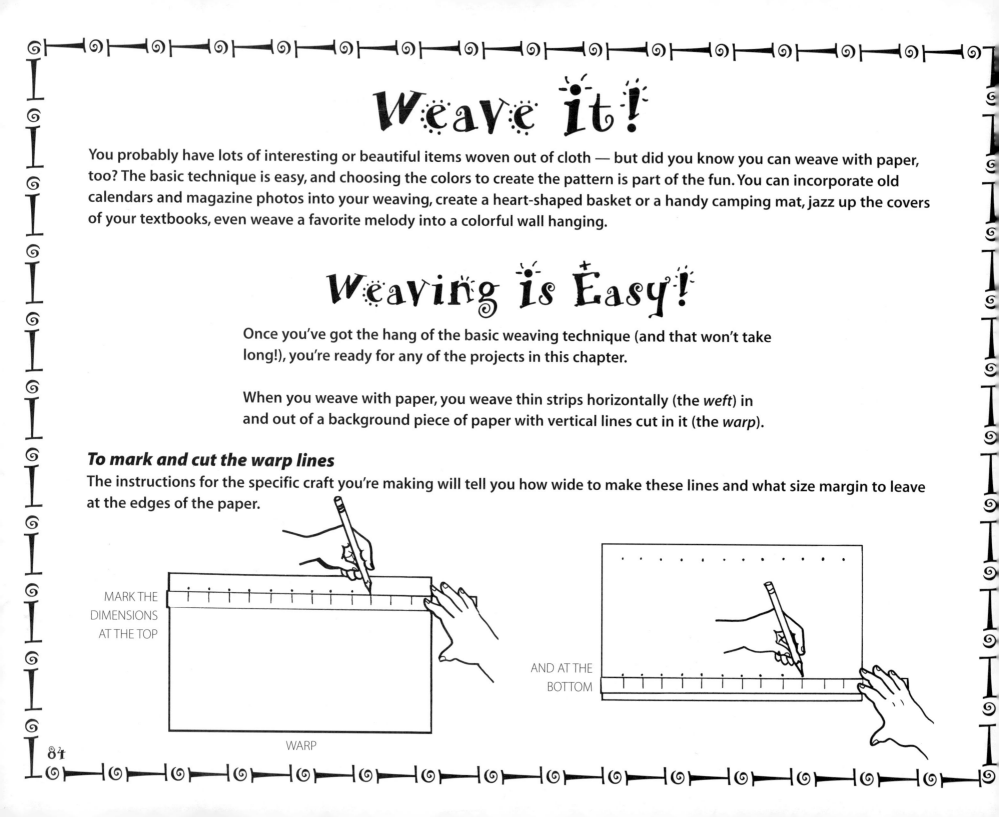

MARK THE DIMENSIONS AT THE TOP

WARP

AND AT THE BOTTOM

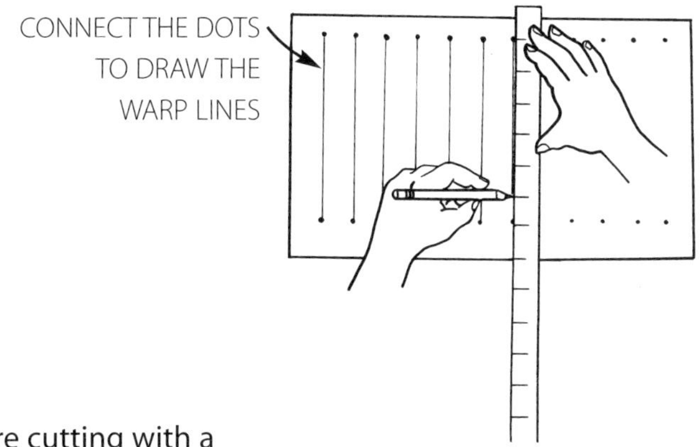

CONNECT THE DOTS
TO DRAW THE
WARP LINES

If you're cutting with a craft knife (page 6), place the warp on a protected surface and use the knife and a ruler to cut from top to bottom *between* the dots.

If you're cutting with scissors, fold the paper in half and cut through the fold line to cut along the warp lines.

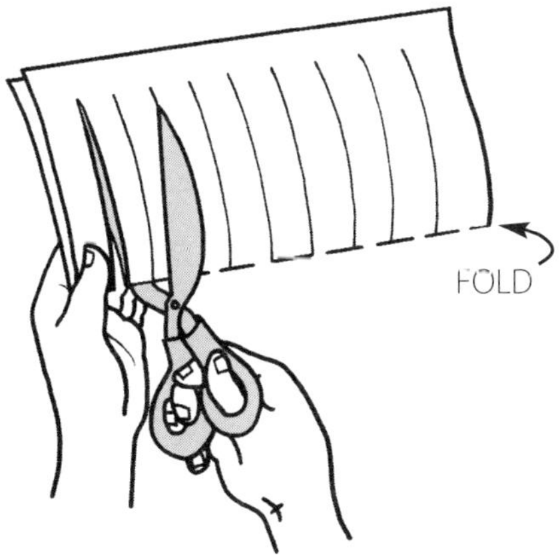

FOLD

To cut the weft strips

See CUTTING TIPS, page 9. Use the width specified in the instructions.

To weave the weft strips

Place your warp paper on a flat surface so the warp lines run top to bottom.

To weave, you pass the weft strip in and out of the warp. You can either start by going over the warp, as show here, or under the warp.

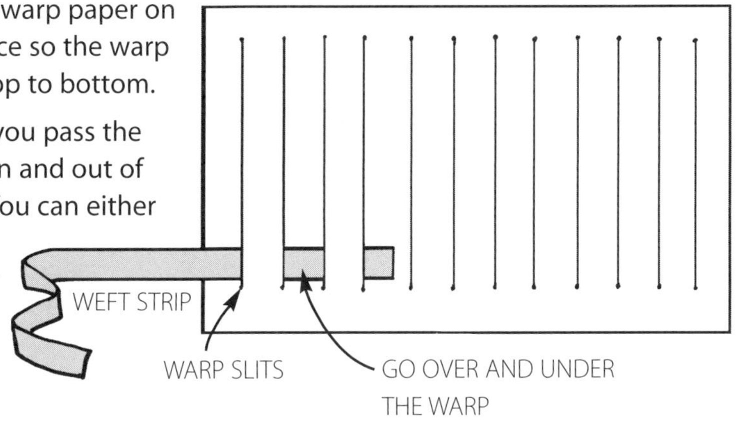

WEFT STRIP

WARP SLITS

GO OVER AND UNDER
THE WARP

When you reach the edge, slide the strip to the bottom of the warp.

To weave the second strip, reverse the pattern. If you started by going over the warp, start the second strip by going under, as shown here.

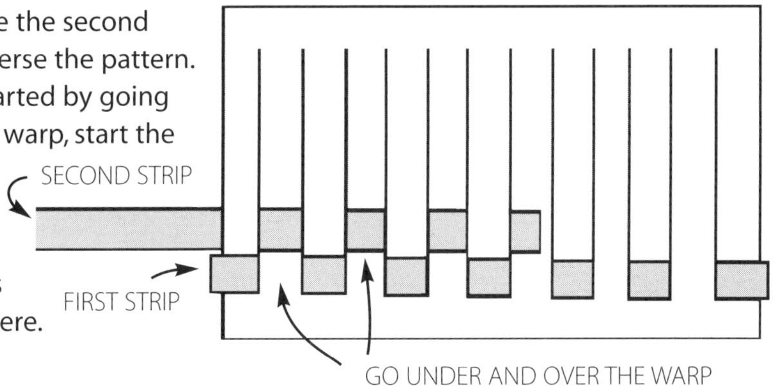

SECOND STRIP

FIRST STRIP

GO UNDER AND OVER THE WARP

Continue weaving the strips, alternating as shown above, until you have filled the warp. Push each new strip up against the preceding one to make the weaving tight.

Colorful Bookmark

Giving a friend a book for his or her birthday? A handmade bookmark is the perfect finishing touch. A small, easy-to-finish bookmark is a fun way to experiment with different color combinations while you practice your weaving skills. (It's also a great way to use up scraps of bright-colored paper left over from other projects.)

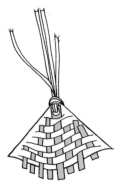

What you need

- Ruler
- Pencil
- Card stock, in assorted colors
- Craft knife (page 6)
- Old newspaper or a piece of thick cardboard
- Glue
- Hole punch
- Yarn or ribbon, 10" (25 cm)

What you do

1. Cut (page 9) a bookmark out of the card stock. Try a 1½" x 5" (3.5 x 12.5 cm) rectangle, a 2½" (6 cm) square, or a small triangle.

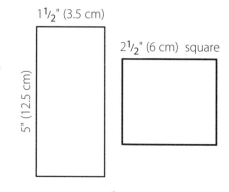

1½" (3.5 cm)

5" (12.5 cm)

2½" (6 cm) square

3" (7.5 cm)   3" (7.5 cm)

5" (12.5 cm)

2. Draw warp lines (page 85) about ¼" (5 mm) from the edges. They can be straight or curvy. Use the craft knife to cut the lines.

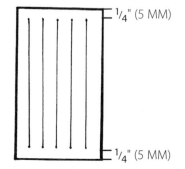

¼" (5 MM)

¼" (5 MM)

3. For the square or triangle, cut ¼" x 5" (5 mm x 12.5 cm) weft strips (page 85) in an assortment of colors. Cut 6" (15 cm) weft strips for the rectangle.

4. Arrange the weft strips until you have a pattern that you like. Lay out the strips in that order, then weave (page 85) them in place. Lightly glue the ends to the warp.

5. Punch a hole in the corner of the shape where you want the tassel to hang. Fold several lengths of yarn or ribbon in half and pass the folded ends through the punched hole.

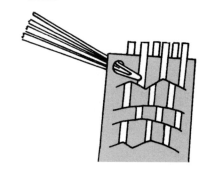

Pass the ends through the loop to form a knot. Pull tight.

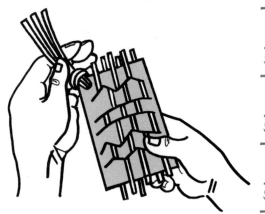

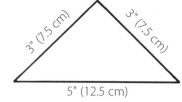

Ocean Waves Greeting Card

Choose patterned paper or cutout pictures in colors that remind you of the ocean. Then, weave them in curving lines like ocean waves!

What you need

- Card stock, 6" x 10" (15 x 25 cm)
- Bone paper folder or Popsicle stick (page 6)
- Ruler
- Craft knife (page 6) or scissors
- Old newspapers or a thick piece of cardboard (optional)
- Decorative paper in blues and greens
- Glue
- Solid-color lightweight paper, 6" x 10" (15 x 25 cm)

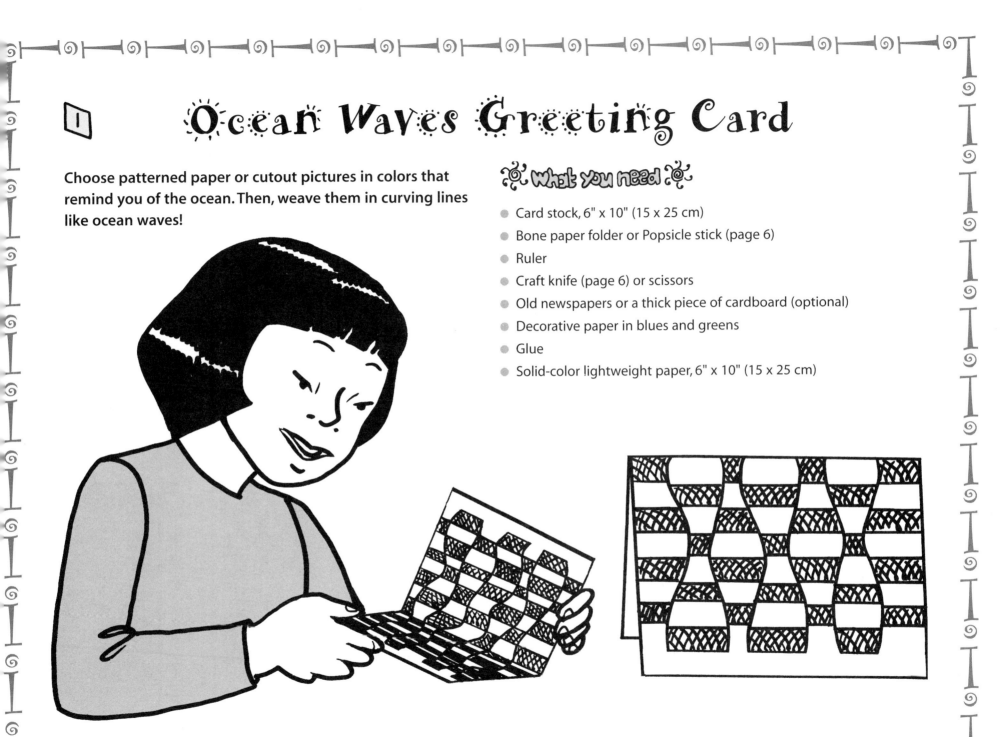

✿ what you do ✿

1. Fold (page 7) the card stock in half, short sides together. Open the fold; turn the paper over.

2. Leaving a ¹/₂" (1 cm) margin on all sides of the card, cut a warp (page 85) of about six wavy lines. Vary the distance between the lines.

10" (25 CM)

6" (15 CM)

¹/₂" (1 CM)

WAVY WARP LINES

CENTER FOLD LINE

3. From the decorative paper, cut weft strips (page 85) about ¹/₂" (1 cm) in width and 8" (20 cm) long.

4. Weave the weft strips (page 85) in an alternating pattern (they will extend slightly beyond the edges of the card). Make sure that a weft strip does not sit directly over the fold in the card.

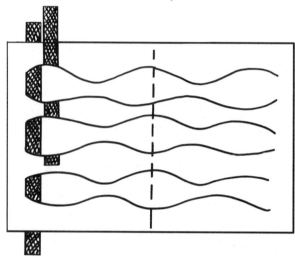

5. Trim the strips evenly to match the edges of the card. Glue the ends to the card to secure them.

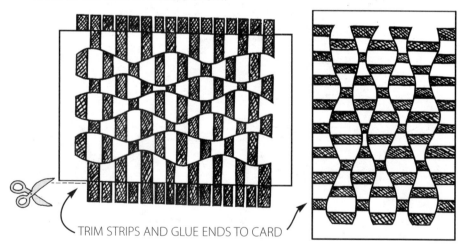

TRIM STRIPS AND GLUE ENDS TO CARD

6. Fold the lightweight paper in half, short sides together. Glue it inside the card for your writing surface.

Favorite-Calendar Place Mat

12

Ever wonder what to do with all those calendars at the end of the year? Weave them into place mats! Ask neighbors and friends to save the pictures from large designer calendars for you. Then use this cool technique to interweave two different pictures together. Pictures with contrasting light and dark areas work best. You can make a set of six matching place mats from one 12-month calendar.

What you need

- Large calendar pictures, two per mat
- Ruler
- Pencil
- Craft knife (page 6) or scissors
- Old newspapers or a thick piece of thick cardboard (optional)
- Glue

1. Choose one picture for the background, or warp (page 84). Cut warp lines as shown.

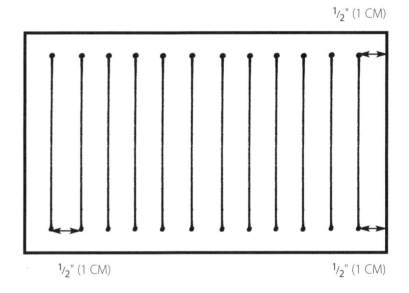

½" (1 CM)

½" (1 CM)   ½" (1 CM)

2. Cut ½" (1 cm) weft strips (page 85) from the long edge of the other picture.

3. Weave (page 85) the weft strips through the warp.

4. Adjust and line up the edges of the strips. Glue along the edges.

Finishing Touches

☀ **LAMINATE OR COVER** the place mat with contact paper to make it waterproof.

Metallic-Weave Planter

This brightly colored planter is perfect for a Mother's Day or spring birthday gift. Include a seed packet of your favorite flowers. Or, make a planter to brighten your own windowsill!

What you do

1. Examine the cup. There are probably several ridges running around it at the top and bottom. You'll need to cut the warp lines (page 85) between these ridges but not through them, or the cup may tear. Don't cut through the rim of your cup.

Cutting the cup with the craft knife is a little tricky; please ask a grown-up for help. Hold the cup firmly against a table with one hand across the top (I like to rest one edge of the cup on the table so I'm cutting on an angle rather than straight up and down). Make cuts about a finger width apart.

If you have a set of ridges in the middle of the cup, stagger the second set of lines so the cup remains strong.

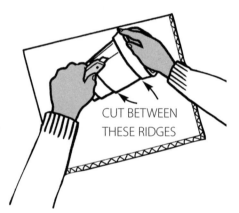

CUT BETWEEN THESE RIDGES

What you need

- 16 oz (500 ml) plastic cup
- Craft knife (page 6)
- Old newspapers or a piece of thick cardboard
- Metallic twist ties, six or seven
- Potting soil
- Flower bulb or seeds

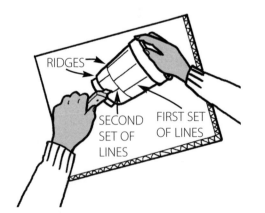

RIDGES

SECOND SET OF LINES

FIRST SET OF LINES

2. Working from bottom to top, weave (page 85) the metallic twist ties as the weft.

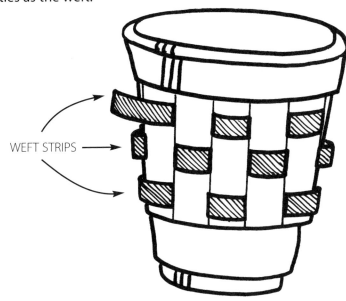

WEFT STRIPS →

3. Trim the twist ties to fit, then overlap the ends and secure as shown.

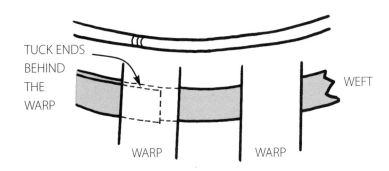

TUCK ENDS BEHIND THE WARP

WARP   WARP

WEFT

4. Fill the cup with potting soil and plant a bulb or several seeds. Keep the soil moist. Place in a sunny window and watch your plant grow!

More Weaving Fun!

It's party time! How about making party-favor baskets for your friends? After they've enjoyed the goodies inside, they can use the basket to hold jewelry, hair ornaments, or pencils.

Choose a paper cup with a decorative pattern and cut paper strips in a matching color. Glue on a narrow strip of paper for the handle at the top of the cup. Slide the ends down through the weft strips on the inside of the cup. Press firmly; let dry. Then, fill with treats!

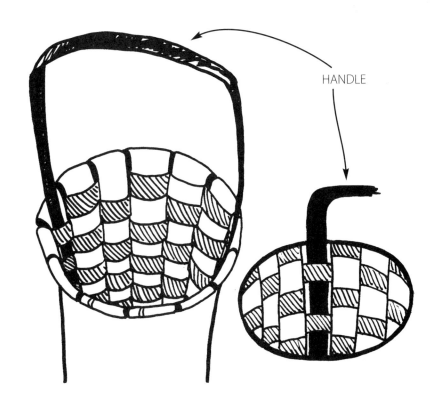

HANDLE

Swedish Heart Basket

Heart baskets are traditionally woven from reed and hung from trees at Christmastime in the Scandinavian countries. Here's a version that can be made from any paper that doesn't tear easily. The weaving is tricky at first, but once you get the hang of it, you'll find these little baskets have lots of uses: May baskets, party favors, a closet sachet, or as "wrapping" for a special little gift.

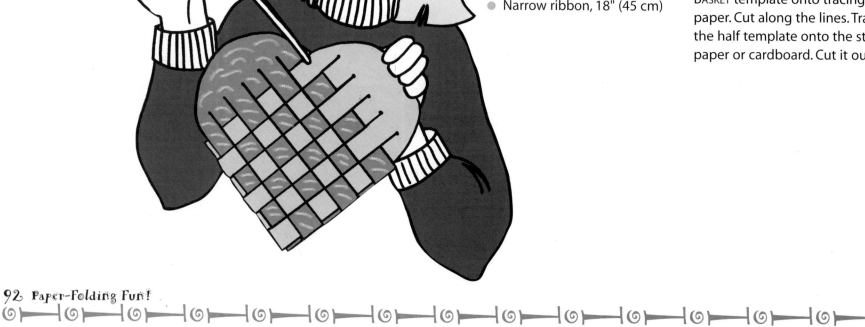

What you need

- *Template-making supplies:* tracing paper, pencil, ruler, craft knife (page 6) or scissors, stiff paper or lightweight cardboard
- Old newspapers or piece of thick cardboard
- Bone paper folder or Popsicle stick (page 6)
- Card stock, two 3½" x 11" (8.5 x 27.5 cm) pieces in contrasting colors
- Narrow ribbon, 18" (45 cm)

What you do

To make the template

If you're cutting out the template with a craft knife, trace the entire HEART BASKET template (page 119) onto tracing paper. Cut along the outside lines. Use the ruler to help you cut along the center lines. Trace the template onto the stiff paper or cardboard. Cut it out.

To cut out the template using scissors, trace half the HEART BASKET template onto tracing paper. Cut along the lines. Trace the half template onto the stiff paper or cardboard. Cut it out.

To cut out the basket

To cut out using a craft knife, trace the full cardboard template onto a piece of card stock. Cut on all the lines. Fold the card stock in half. Repeat with the other piece of card stock.

To cut out using scissors, fold a piece of card stock in half. Trace the "half" cardboard template onto the card stock as shown.

Trace all lines. Cut through both pieces of card stock. Repeat with the other piece of card stock.

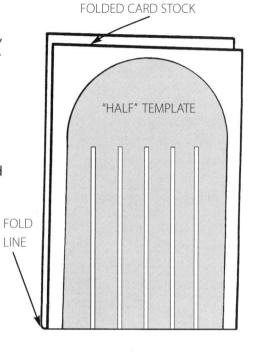

FOLDED CARD STOCK

"HALF" TEMPLATE

FOLD LINE

To weave the basket together

This part will take some time, so relax and enjoy it!

1. Hold one folded basket section in your left hand with the slits pointing up. These will be the A strips.

Hold the other folded section in your right hand. These will be the B strips. Hold them at right angles to the A strips. You're actually holding the basket upside down while you weave it.

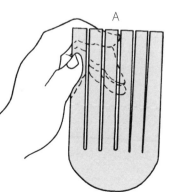

A

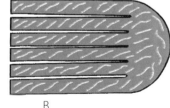

B

2. To weave the two sections together, you go *through* the strips, rather than over and under them. Here's the pattern:

To weave the first B strip:

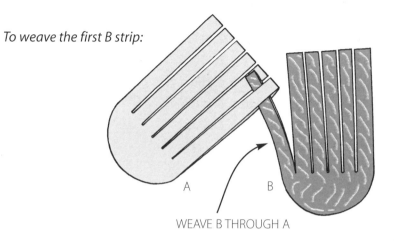

A   B

WEAVE B THROUGH A

THEN WEAVE A THROUGH B

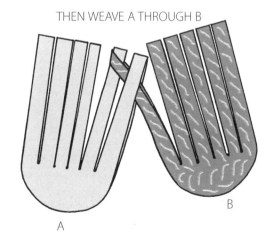

A   B

Repeat to the end of the B strip. If you have trouble remembering the pattern, try repeating it out loud, "B through A, A through B," while you weave.

3. Now reverse the pattern.

WEAVE
A THROUGH B

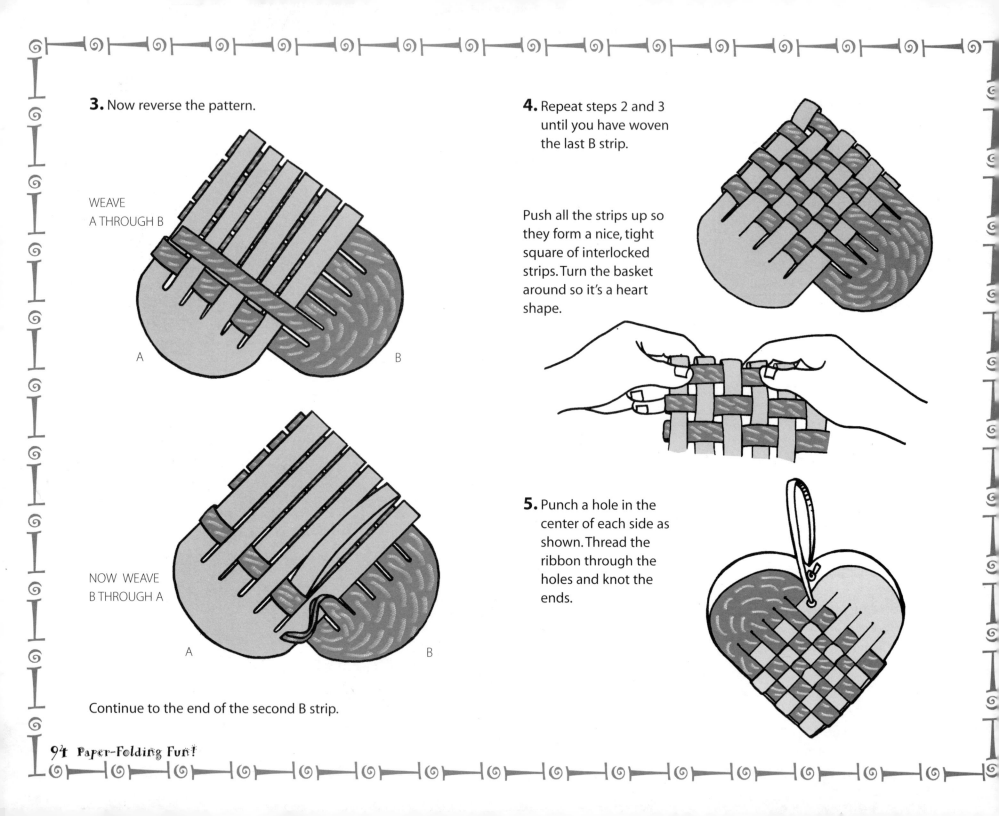

A   B

NOW WEAVE
B THROUGH A

A   B

Continue to the end of the second B strip.

4. Repeat steps 2 and 3 until you have woven the last B strip.

Push all the strips up so they form a nice, tight square of interlocked strips. Turn the basket around so it's a heart shape.

5. Punch a hole in the center of each side as shown. Thread the ribbon through the holes and knot the ends.

Weave a Melody!

Even if you don't know how to play a single note, you can create this colorful wall hanging that actually displays a melody! Each horizontal strip represents one note in the old favorite "Mary Had a Little Lamb." Once you learn the technique, you can transform any simple tune into a work of art. (If you need help with the notes, ask a grown-up or friend who reads music.)

Four Notes, Four Colors

"Mary Had a Little Lamb" has four notes: E, D, C, and G.

Each syllable or word gets one note. You'll choose a color for each note and, starting at the top, weave a strip of that color into the background paper, just as if you're singing the song.

Ma-ry	had	a	lit-tle	lamb,	lit-tle	lamb,	lit-tle	lamb
E D	C	D	E E	E	D D	D	E G	G

Ma-ry	had	a	lit-tle	lamb,	its	fleece	was	white	as	snow.
E D	C	D	E E	E	D	D	E	D	C

what you need

- Card stock: four 4" x 11" (10 x 27.5 cm) strips in bright colors; 9" x 12" (22.5 x 30 cm) piece in a contrasting color for the background
- Pencil
- Ruler
- Craft knife (page 6) or scissors
- Old newspapers or piece of thick cardboard (optional)
- Hole punch
- Ribbon, 12" (30 cm)

what you do

1. Assign a color of card stock to each note (see box). Cut (page 9) each color into ¼" x 11" (5 mm x 27.5 cm) strips. These will be the weft strips (page 85). You will need 11 of color E, 10 of color D, three of color C, and two of color G.

2. Draw warp lines (page 85) in the background card stock, leaving a ½" (1 cm) margin on each long side and a 1" (2.5 cm) margin at the top and bottom.

3. To cut the warp lines with a craft knife, draw additional lines between these two outside lines. The lines may be wavy or straight. On a protected surface, cut along the lines.

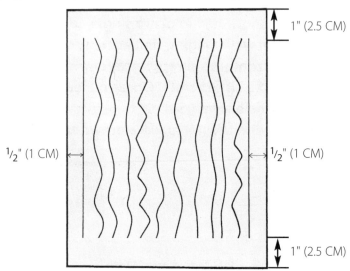

If using scissors, fold the background paper in half, short sides together. Draw lines from the fold up.

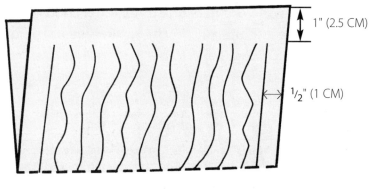

FOLD LINE

Cut through the fold line to cut along each warp line. Unfold the paper.

4. For the title, cut a strip of paper about $^3/_4$" (2 cm) wide and 11" (27.5 cm) long. Weave (page 85) it across the top (you may have to lengthen the cut lines to make room). Write the name of the song on the strip (see illustration of finished weaving, page 95).

5. Lay the background paper flat. Beginning at the top, weave the colored strips, following the color pattern of the melody (see box, page 95). It may help to sing along as you weave! Try it!

6. Punch two holes at the top of the paper. Thread the ribbon through and tie. Turn the ribbon until the knot is hidden at the back of the weaving. Lightly glue the ends of the strips to the edges of the warp to hold them in place.

STRIP
FOR TITLE

Mʌ- (E)

-RY (D)

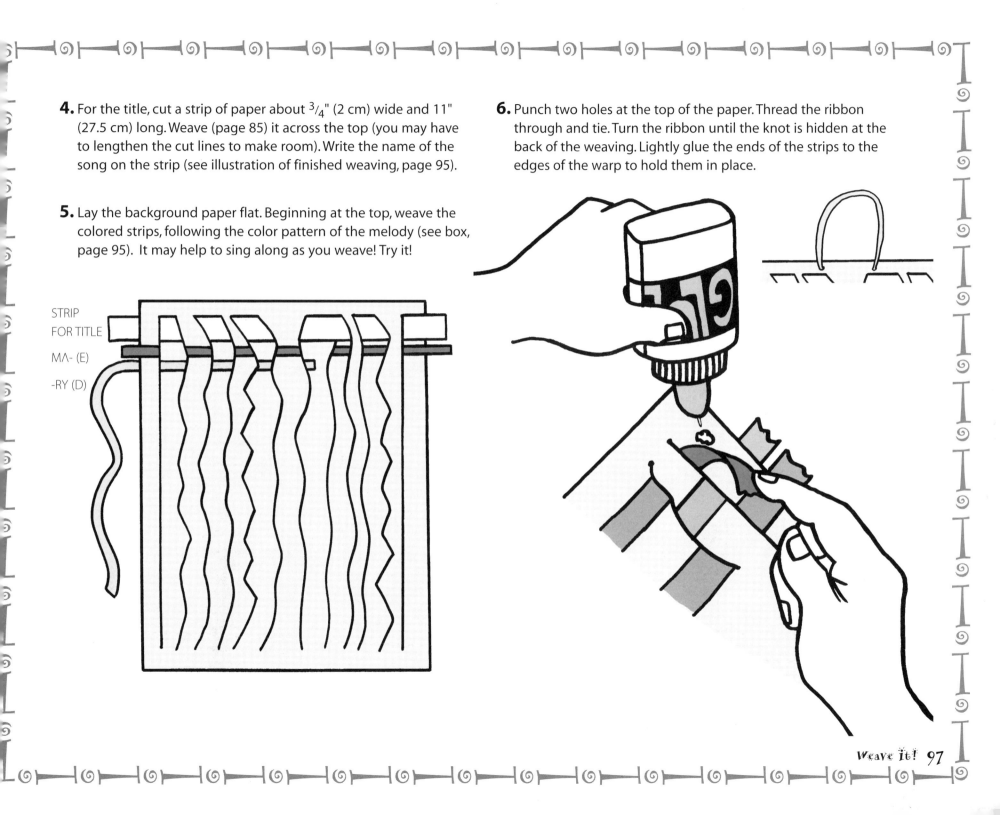

Sit-Upon Mat

No more worries about sitting on wet grass with your very own woven mat! It's also handy for damp picnic benches and for sitting around the campfire on a cool night. Your finished mat will be about 12" x 14½" (30 x 36 cm) in size. And you'll be amazed at how sturdy it is with no glue — only your weaving holds it together. So start saving those Sunday funnies!

⚘ What you need ⚘

● 14 four-page sections of old newspaper
● Ruler
● Scissors

❀ What you do ❀

1. Fold a section of newspaper in half, long sides together. Fold it again in the same way. Continue folding in this way until the strip is about 1¾" (4.5 cm) wide.

1¾" (4.5 CM)

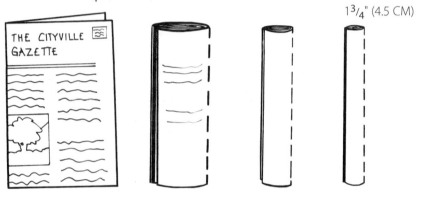

KEEP FOLDING THE STRIP IN HALF

Repeat with the other 13 sections of newspaper.

2. Place eight of the strips on a flat surface as shown. These will form the warp (page 84).

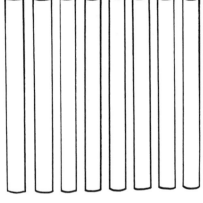

WARP STRIPS

3. The six remaining strips are the weft (page 84). Weave (page 85) the weft strips through the warp, starting about 5" (12.5 cm) from the bottom.

5" (12.5 CM)

5" (12.5 CM)

4. Your mat may look slightly out of shape. Straighten the strips until you see a woven rectangle in the center of your project. Push the strips close together so there are no gaps between them.

Trim each warp and weft strip to be about 4" (10 cm) beyond the woven section.

TRIM TO
4" (10 CM)

4" (10 CM)

4" (10 CM)

4" (10 CM)

5. Beginning at the bottom right edge of the mat, fold each warp strip extending from the underside of the mat up and around the weft strip, and tuck the end in behind the strip.

Continue across the bottom edge of the mat. You will be working with every other strip.

FOLD AROUND AND TUCK IN

BOTTOM OF MAT

6. Turn the mat so the top is now at the bottom. Continue to fold the strips that extend from the underside up and over as shown in step 5 to secure them.

Repeat on each side.

TOP

BOTTOM

7. Flip your mat over and repeat the process to tuck the remaining strips into the back side. You may have to adjust the corners.

8. Decorate the four corners by tracing the APPLE template (page 117) and using it as a pattern to cut the shape out of stiff paper. Cover the apples with clear contact paper before gluing them in place. Great job! Now have a seat!

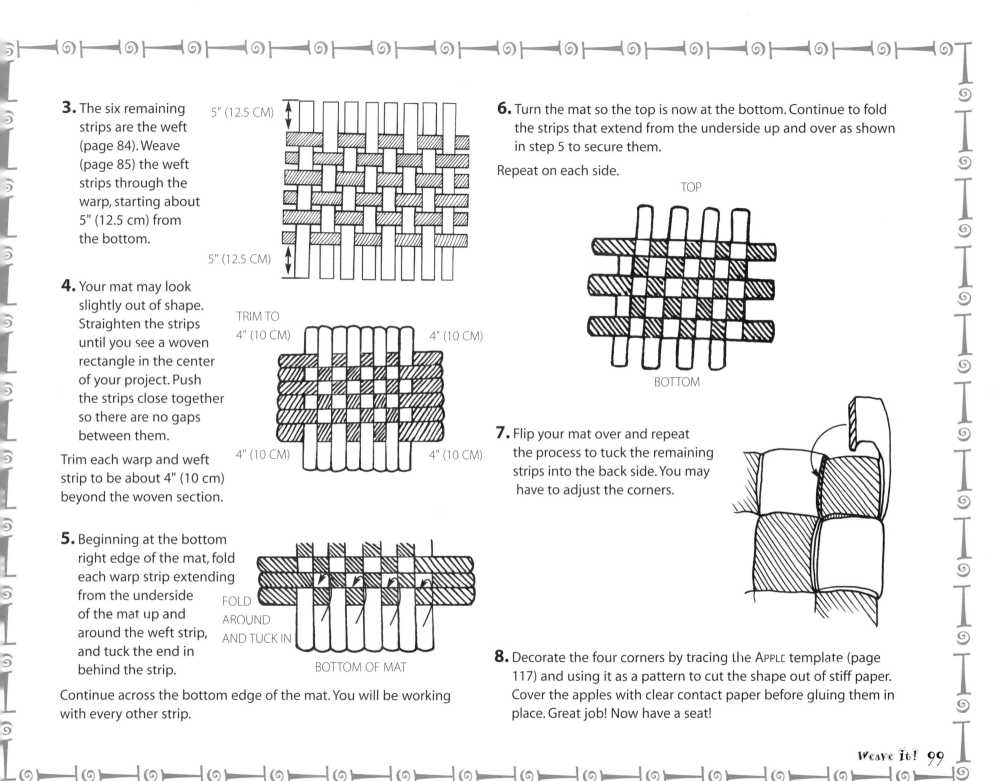

Personalized Book Cover

No more boring brown paper book covers! Now you can design a unique cover for each of your schoolbooks using various weaving techniques. Use "window weaving" to let bright colors show through cutout sections of the bag. Try a technique I call "structural weaving" to create a 3-D effect. Add other techniques from this book as finishing touches. Then, cover your work of art with clear contact paper to protect it, if you like.

Maybe you'll start a new trend at school! How about a "book cover" party to teach the art of making these one-of-a-kind versions?

What you need

- Book cover made from a brown paper grocery bag (see page 101)
- Scissors
- Bone paper folder or Popsicle stick (page 6)
- Pencil
- Craft knife (page 6)
- Old newspapers or a piece of thick cardboard
- Bright, solid-colored, metallic, or decorative paper; gift wrap; cutout pictures from magazines
- Glue
- Gel pens or markers

To make a book cover

Need a refresher on making a book cover from a paper bag? Here you go!

1. Cut down one side of the bag, along a fold line. Cut off the bottom of the bag.

2. Place the book on the unfolded bag. Fold (page 7) the bag along the top and bottom edges of the book.

3. Fold the left side of the bag over about 4" (10 cm). Slip the front cover of the book into this flap.

FOLD DOWN

FOLD UP

4" (10 CM)

FOLD LINE

4. Wrap the cover tightly around the book. Fold the right side of the paper cover around the back cover of the book, cutting off some of the bag if necessary. Slip the back cover into the flap. Adjust so the book cover fights tightly.

BACK SIDE OF
LAST PAGE
OF BOOK

INSIDE OF
BACK COVER

✿ What you do ✿

1. With the cover on the book, write the title in pencil. Remove the cover. Open the cover on all fold lines and place, right side up, on a protected surface. Keep all your decorating within these fold lines.

With the craft knife, cut a large opening around the title of the book. Choose a bright-colored paper and glue it to the inside of the book cover so it shows through the opening. Use markers to write the title and decorate around it.

2. For *"structural weaving"*: Cut a small shape in the cover, leaving one edge attached. Cut two parallel lines. Weave the shape through the lines as shown. Glue metallic or other bright-colored paper behind the opening left by the shape.

CUTOUT SHAPE

FOLD

CUT LINES

WEAVE THE SHAPE THROUGH THE SLITS

3. For *"window weaving"*: Mark several 3" (7.5 cm) squares on the bag. Cut different types of openings in these "windows." Cut along two or three sides of the figures and fold back the flaps in different ways. Glue in place.

3" (7.5 CM)

CUT ON DARK LINES

FOLD ON DOTTED LINES

Glue magazine pictures or squares of decorative or gift wrap to the back side of the bag so they show through the window openings.

4. For *traditional weaving:* Cut four or five long zigzag warp strips (page 84) on the cover. Weave (page 85) bright-colored weft strips through these strips. Glue the ends.

Glue on a piece of decorative paper first, if you like, and cut slits for weaving in that (see oval in the center of the finished book cover).

5. Look through this book for other decorating ideas. How about one of the kaleidoscope origami designs (page 80), such as the one shown in the upper corner of the finished cover, or a quilled flower (page 38)?

6. Decorate with words, sayings, and "doodles" between your weavings and other decorations. And don't forget to sign your cover with your best artist's signature!

Box it!

Don't you just love peeking inside a small box to see what's inside? Boxes are perfect for small gifts and for storing beads, sea glass, hair ornaments, and other treasures. Now, you can make your own out of your favorite papers. Several of the boxes in this chapter are especially magical because they are held together only by the folds — no tape or glue needed! Several are made with a template, which you can enlarge on a copier to make the boxes any size you want. When you're making a box, it's especially important to cut carefully and firmly crease all fold lines so it has a precise shape.

Beginner Box

This box is a favorite with beginners because it's easy and foolproof. It's great fun to write a letter to a relative and enclose a flattened box with directions for refolding!

Practice making the box with scrap paper first. You'll quickly master the folds, and then you can try different-weight papers. The larger the box, the stronger the paper should be to maintain the shape.

what you need

- Card stock, 8½" x 11" (21 x 27.5 cm) for a 4¼" x 5½" (10.5 x 13.5 cm) finished box
- Bone paper folder or Popsicle stick (page 6)

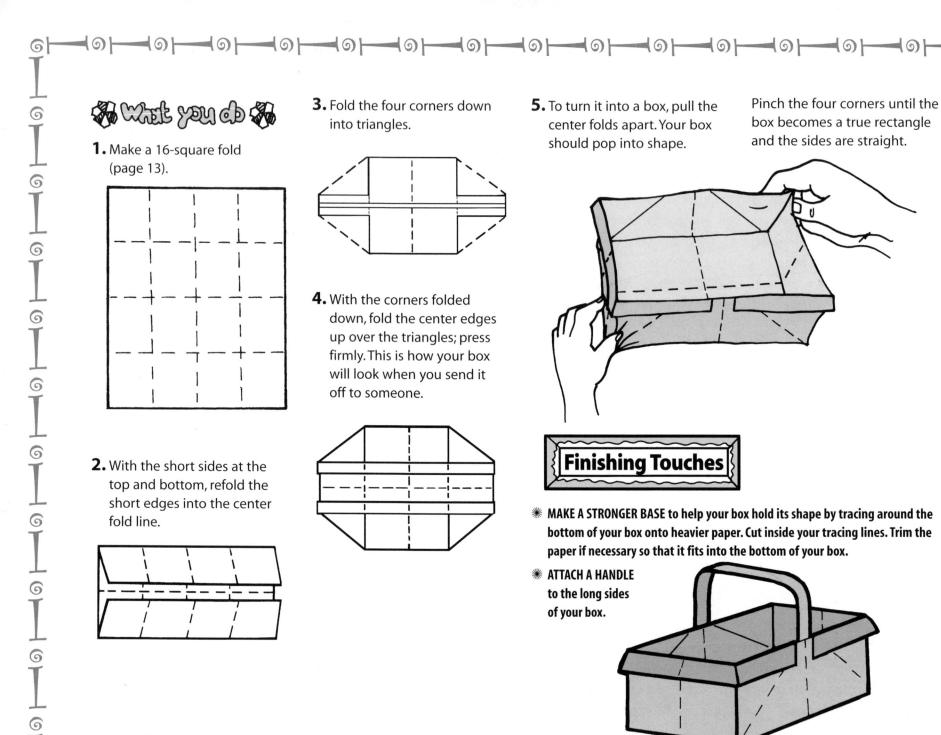

❀ What you do ❀

1. Make a 16-square fold (page 13).

2. With the short sides at the top and bottom, refold the short edges into the center fold line.

3. Fold the four corners down into triangles.

4. With the corners folded down, fold the center edges up over the triangles; press firmly. This is how your box will look when you send it off to someone.

5. To turn it into a box, pull the center folds apart. Your box should pop into shape.

Pinch the four corners until the box becomes a true rectangle and the sides are straight.

Finishing Touches

❋ **MAKE A STRONGER BASE** to help your box hold its shape by tracing around the bottom of your box onto heavier paper. Cut inside your tracing lines. Trim the paper if necessary so that it fits into the bottom of your box.

❋ **ATTACH A HANDLE** to the long sides of your box.

Matchbox Necklace

see photograph,
back cover

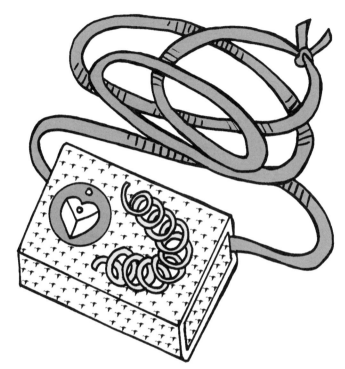

How about a necklace with a secret drawer? This box can hold a tiny book, a special piece of jewelry, pictures of friends, or other small treasures like tiny shells or a favorite piece of sea glass. Pair it with the MINI-BOOK CHARM BRACELET on page 23. Who knows — you just might start a new fad at school!

What you need

- Empty matchbox, $1^3/_8$" x $2^1/_8$" (3.5 x 5 cm)
- Small paintbrush
- Glue
- Decorative paper, $2^1/_8$" x $4^1/_2$" (5 x 11 cm); plus a scrap in the same pattern
- Pencil
- Ribbon or yarn, 34" (85 cm)
- Beads, glitter, gel pens, sequins, and other decorations

What you do

1. Remove the drawer from the matchbox. Brush glue over the outside of the matchbox. Beginning at the edge of one large side, wrap the decorative paper around the box. Overlap ends and press firmly. Let dry.

OVERLAP ENDS

2. Place the drawer on the scrap of decorative paper as shown. Trace around the ends and cut out.

TRACE TWO
TIMES AND
CUT OUT

Cover the two outside ends of the drawer with glue and press the end papers in place. Let dry.

3. Slide the length of ribbon or yarn through the box top and knot the ends.

More Folding Fun!

Put a tiny book inside

1. With a $4^3/_4$" x $7^1/_2$" (12 x 18.5 cm) piece of lightweight paper, make a 16-SQUARE ACCORDION BOOK (page 20).

2. Glue the folded book into the box. Extend the book pages until the glue dries.

3. Write a message on the book pages and refold into the box.

Use as party favors. Write your friends' names on the cover with glitter glue and slip a favorite treat inside.

Small-as-Can-Be Box

This little box is the perfect gift box for a pair of earrings, or it can hold a special mini-card for a friend who needs cheering up. It's great for storing paper clips, tiny buttons, or favorite beads, too.

It's also my favorite way to recycle old cards — I use the front of the printed side for the top.

What you need

- *Template-making supplies:* tracing paper, pencil, ruler, scissors, stiff paper or lightweight cardboard
- Card stock, a little larger than the templates
- Bone paper folder or Popsicle stick (page 6)

What you do

To make the templates

Trace the SMALL-AS-CAN-BE BOX TOP and SMALL-AS-CAN-BE BOX BOTTOM templates (page 120) onto tracing paper. Mark all score and cut lines. Cut them out.

Trace onto stiff paper or cardboard. Transfer all markings. Cut out the templates.

To make the box

1. Trace the templates onto the card stock. Transfer all markings.

2. Cut out the boxes. Score (page 8) on all score lines. Cut on cut lines.

3. To make the box bottom: fold (page 7) up the four corner flaps.

FOLD FLAPS UP

BOX BOTTOM

Fold the side pieces in. You should see a square that is the bottom of the box.

4. Fold the shorter side up and over the sides of your box, tucking the crease down into the fold at the bottom of the box.

Fold the longer side in the same way so that the last flap becomes the bottom of the box.

THEN FOLD THIS SIDE IN

FOLD THIS SIDE IN

5. Repeat these steps to fold the box top.

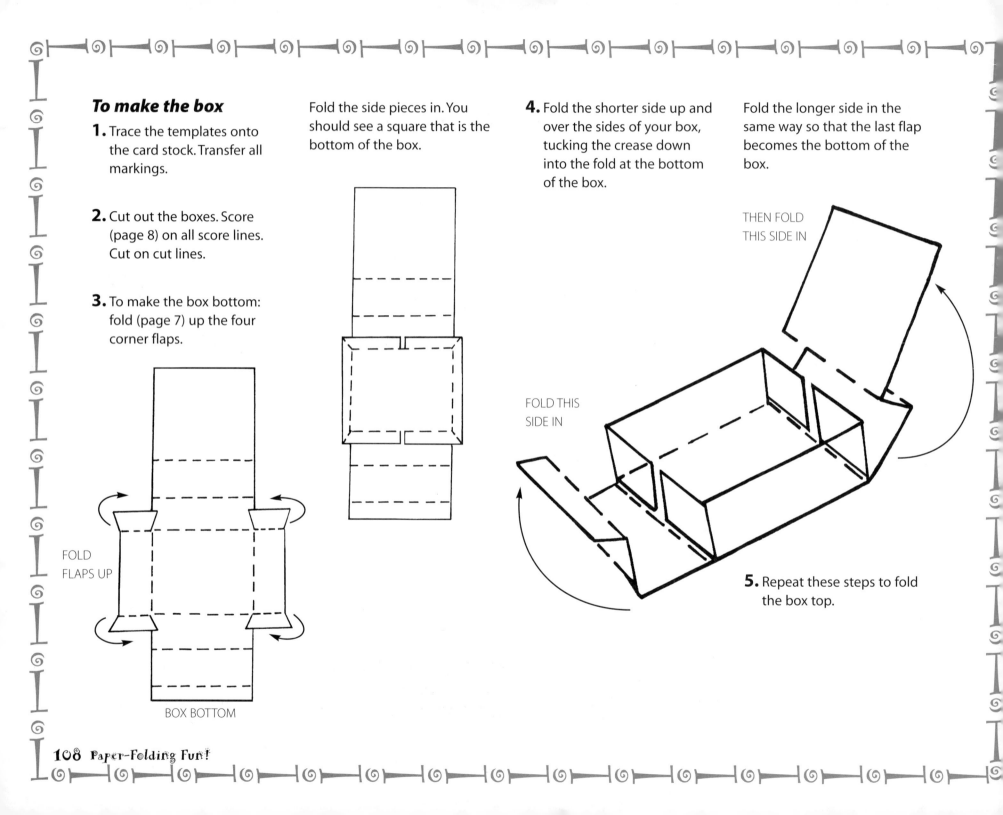

Flat Box with Lid

This easy-to-make box is perfect for storing favorite note cards, photos, or messages from a special friend. Or, for a great gift, make a set of kaleidoscope origami note cards (page 83) to go inside.

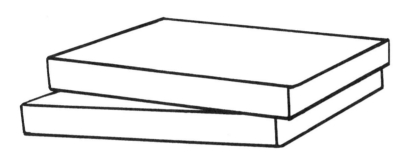

What you need

- *Template-making supplies:* tracing paper, pencil, ruler, scissors, stiff paper or light-weight cardboard
- Card stock, two 6$\frac{1}{2}$" x 7$\frac{1}{2}$" (16 x 18.5 cm) pieces
- Bone paper folder or Popsicle stick (page 6)
- Glue

What you do

To make the templates

Trace the FLAT BOX TOP and FLAT BOX BOTTOM templates (pages 121 and 122) onto the tracing paper, marking all score and cut lines. (They look the same but are slightly different so that the top will fit over the bottom.) Cut them out.

Trace the templates onto the stiff paper or cardboard. Transfer all markings. Cut them out.

To make the box

1. Trace the templates onto the card stock. Transfer all markings and cut them out. Score (page 8) on all score lines.

2. Fold (page 7) up the box bottom on the scored lines to form a shallow box.

3. To make the box ends, fold tabs in and glue end flaps over them.

GLUE FLAPS TO FORM CORNERS

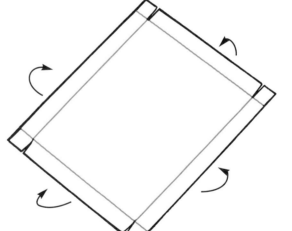

4. Repeat with the box lid.

Finishing Touches

✳ **DECORATE THE LID** with markers or gel pens, sequins, stickers, glitter glue, a kaleidoscope origami (page 80) or other decorations.

Party Favor Mini-Bag

These little bags are not for parties only! At the holidays, I make them from holiday gift wrap, and fill them with tiny pinecones or red and white peppermints and hang them on our Christmas tree. Or, make the bag out of pink or red paper, decorate with heart stickers, and fill with treats for your special valentine! Fold a tiny card to go inside (see MORE FOLDING FUN!, page 106) and tie it to a present.

What you need

- *Template-making supplies:* tracing paper, pencil, ruler, scissors, stiff paper or lightweight cardboard

- Decorative paper, larger than the template

- Bone paper folder or Popsicle stick (page 6)

- Glue

- Small nail or large needle

- Narrow elastic thread or ribbon, 8" (20 cm)

What you do

To make the template

Trace the PARTY FAVOR MINI-BAG template (page 119) onto the tracing paper, marking all score lines. Cut it out.

Trace the tracing-paper template onto the stiff paper or cardboard. Transfer all markings. Cut it out.

To make the bag

1. Trace the cardboard template onto the decorative paper. Transfer all markings and cut it out.

2. Score (page 8) all score lines. Fold (page 7) all scored lines in the same direction.

3. Fold the bag as shown and glue the tab. Let dry.

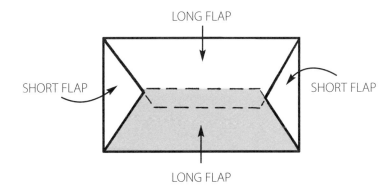

GLUE HERE

4. Fold in the short bottom flaps and fold the longer flaps over them. Glue the last flap in place to form the bottom of the bag.

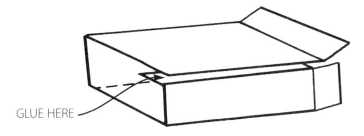

LONG FLAP

SHORT FLAP   SHORT FLAP

LONG FLAP

5. Fold the narrow top edge to the inside of the bag. Glue it in place if you like.

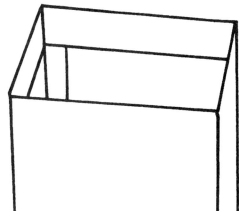

6. With the nail or needle, poke a hole through the top edge of both long sides large enough for the thread or ribbon to pass through. Thread the elastic or ribbon from the outside to the inside of your bag. Knot the two ends on the inside.

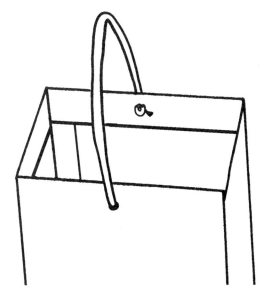

Spiral Box

*see photograph,
front cover*

This is a box and lid all in one!
Instead of four corners, there
are four "waves." Lock them
together to create a spiral
design on top. Decorate the
ends of the waves and you
create a jeweled top! Whip
one up for a friend — and
don't be surprised when
you're asked to make more!

What you need

- *Template-making supplies:*
  tracing paper, pencil, ruler,
  scissors, stiff paper or
  lightweight cardboard
- Card stock, 8½" (21 cm)
  square
- Bone paper folder or
  Popsicle stick (page 6)

What you do

To make the template

Trace the SPIRAL BOX template
(page 123) onto tracing paper,
marking all score lines. Cut it
out.

Trace the tracing-paper template onto the stiff paper or
cardboard. Transfer all markings.
Cut it out.

To make the box

1. Trace the cardboard template onto the card stock. Transfer all score lines. Cut it out.

2. Score (page 8) on the score lines. Fold (page 7) all scored lines in the same direction.

3. Holding "wave" 1 in place, fold and secure the box as shown. You should see a spiral on the top of your box.

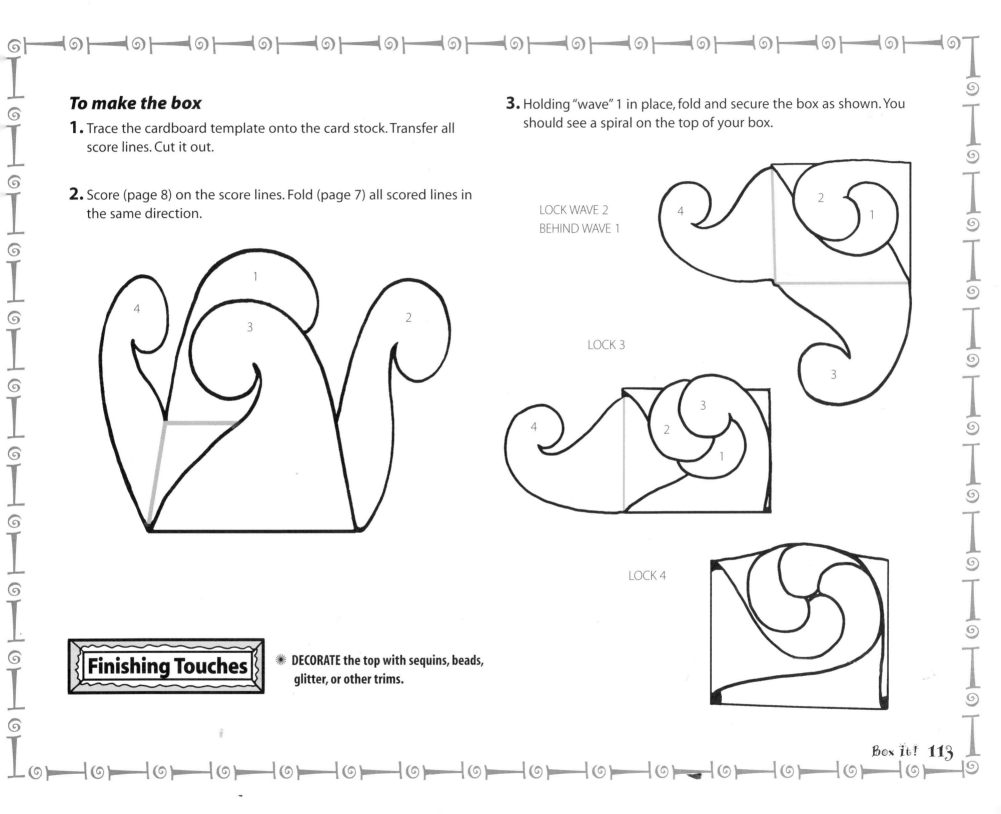

LOCK WAVE 2
BEHIND WAVE 1

LOCK 3

LOCK 4

Finishing Touches

✳ **DECORATE** the top with sequins, beads, glitter, or other trims.

123 Stacked Boxes with Bead Knobs

see photograph, front cover

Have you ever had a set of wooden dolls that stack one inside the other? Well, now you can fold two neat boxes and one fits right inside the other, knob and all! I have several sets that I enjoy just playing with.

OK, yes, it may look like a lot of steps, but most of them are just simple folds. The only tricky part is actually forming the box shape. Follow the illustrations carefully and with just a couple of final folds, you'll see a square box take shape right before your eyes! Pretty cool!

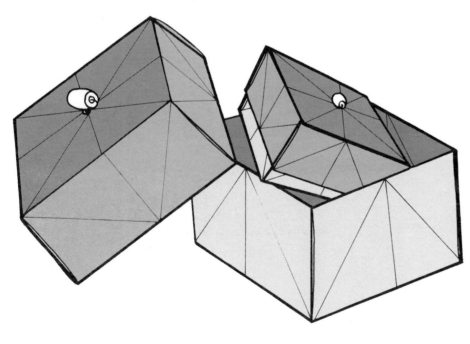

What you need

- Card stock:
  For the large box
- 8" (20 cm) square for the box bottom; 8½" (21 cm) square for the box top; 3" (7.5 cm) square for the box top insert (optional); 2¾" (7cm) square for the box bottom insert (optional)

  For the small box
- 5½" (13.5 cm) square for the box bottom; 6" (15 cm) square for the box top; 2" (5 cm) square for the box bottom and insert (optional)
- Pencil
- Bone paper folder or Popsicle stick (page 6)
- One large and one small bead
- Tape
- Small nail or large needle
- Narrow elastic cording
- Scissors

What you do

To make each box bottom

1. Make the card-stock square for the box bottom into a 16-square fold (page 13).

2. Flip the paper over. Fold the opposite corners together to create a diagonal fold. Open the fold. Repeat on the other diagonal line. Open the fold.

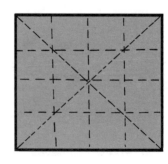

3. Flip the paper over. Fold each corner to the center of the paper. Open the folds.

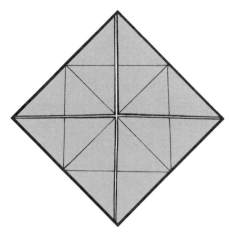

4. Open the folds. Locate the inside square in the middle of the paper as shown. It may help to mark the four corners of this square lightly with pencil, as you will be using them for reference on certain folds.

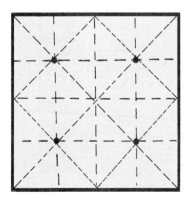

5. Fold an outside corner across the center point to the opposite corner of the inside square that you just marked. Open the fold.

Repeat with the other outside corners.

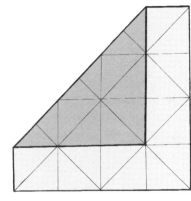

FOLD EACH OUTSIDE CORNER TO THE OPPOSITE CORNER OF THE CENTER SQUARE, THEN OPEN THE FOLD

6. Fold each outside corner into a small triangle as shown, touching the outside point to the corner point of the inside square. Open the folds.

Lightly outline the square in the center. This is the box bottom. The pencil lines will guide you in folding the box.

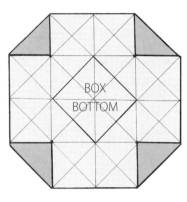

7. To form into a box, position the paper in a diamond shape. Fold two opposite corners to the center point, forming two triangles.

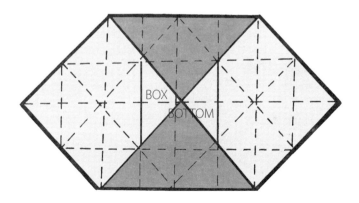

8. Fold the sides of these triangles up to form sides of the box.

9. Pinch in the sides of one extending flap as shown.

Fold the point of the flap over these sides and into the center of the box.

Repeat with the other extending flap.

10. Pinch the corners so the box takes on a square shape. Secure all the inside triangles by pushing the insert into the box bottom.

To make each box top

1. Using the square for the box top, repeat the steps for the box bottom.

2. Before attaching the bead to the small box top, make sure it will fit inside the larger box when the lid is on.

To attach the bead, gently unfold the last two flaps. Reinforce the center of the top with a small piece of tape. With the needle, poke two holes in the center of the top as shown.

POKE HOLES

TAPE

Push one end of the elastic thread through one hole. Thread a bead onto the cording and pass the other end through the other hole.

Knot the thread on the inside of the box top. Refold the flaps.

3. Secure all the inside triangles by pushing the insert into the box top.

Templates

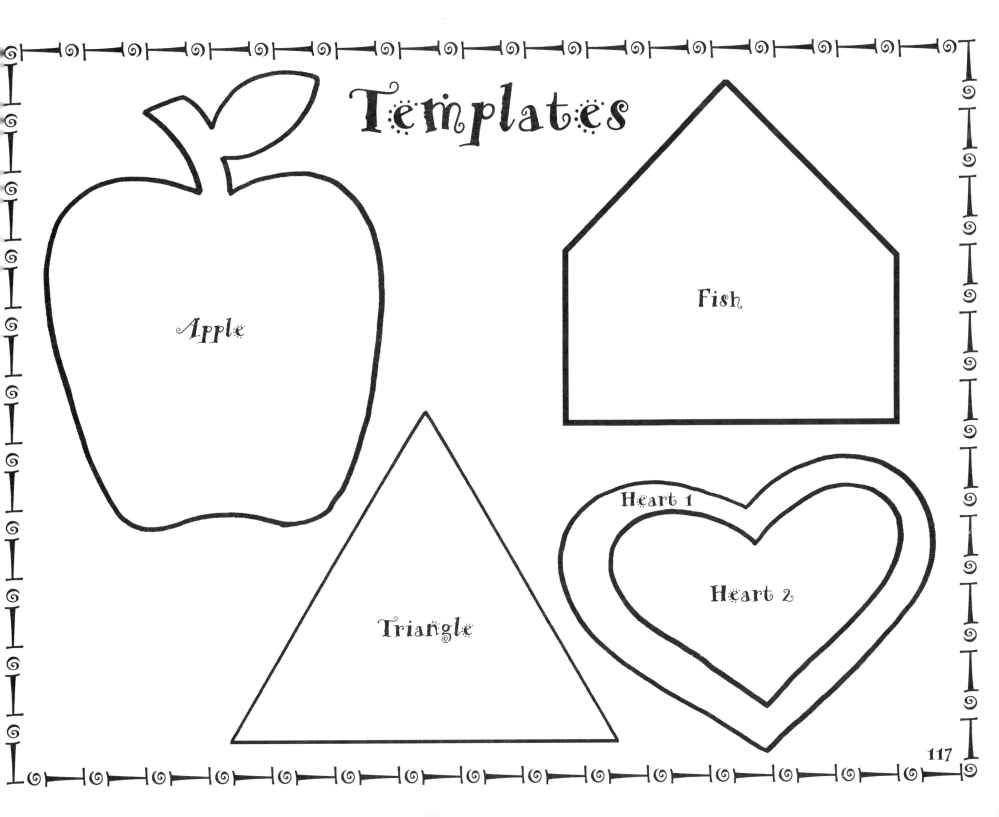

Apple

Fish

Triangle

Heart 1

Heart 2

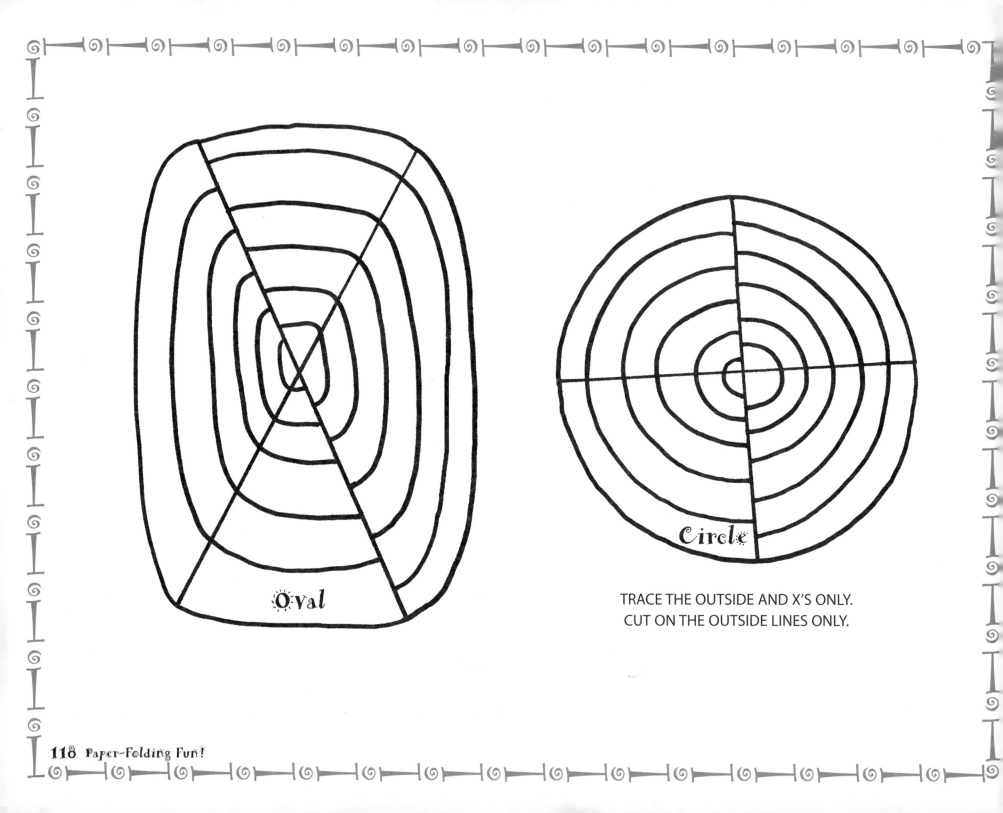

Oval

Circle

TRACE THE OUTSIDE AND X'S ONLY.
CUT ON THE OUTSIDE LINES ONLY.

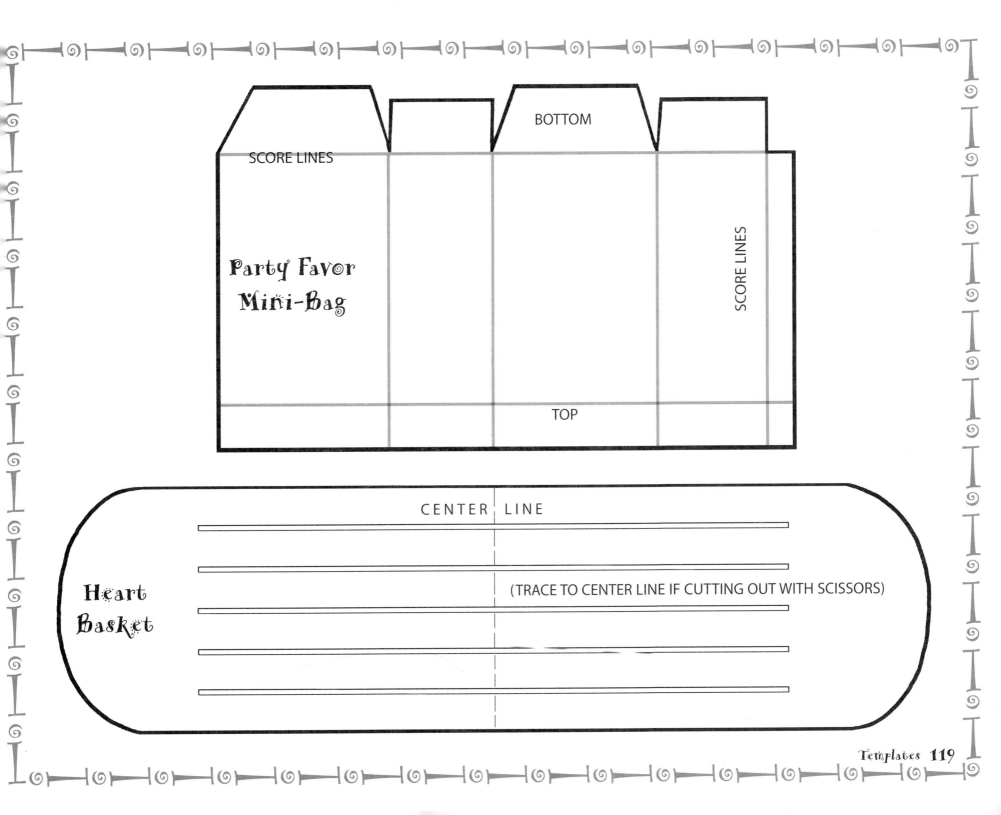

SCORE LINES

BOTTOM

Party Favor
Mini-Bag

SCORE LINES

TOP

CENTER LINE

Heart
Basket

(TRACE TO CENTER LINE IF CUTTING OUT WITH SCISSORS)

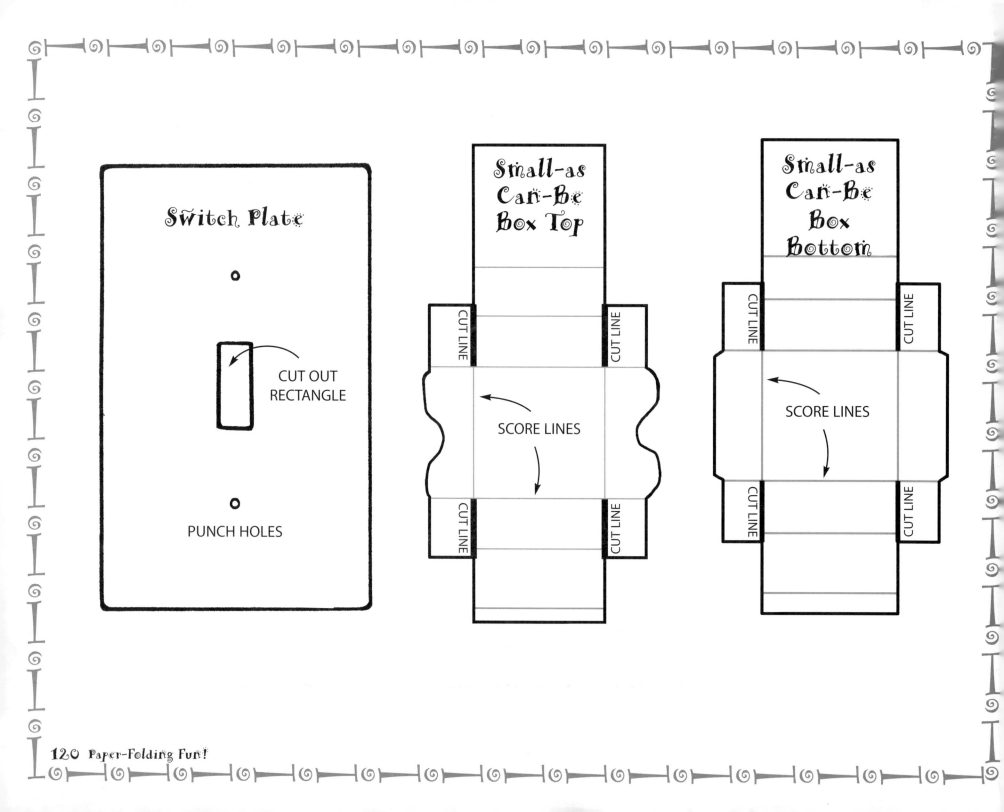

Switch Plate

CUT OUT
RECTANGLE

PUNCH HOLES

Small-as Can-Be Box Top

CUT LINE

CUT LINE

CUT LINE

CUT LINE

SCORE LINES

Small-as Can-Be Box Bottom

CUT LINE

CUT LINE

CUT LINE

CUT LINE

SCORE LINES

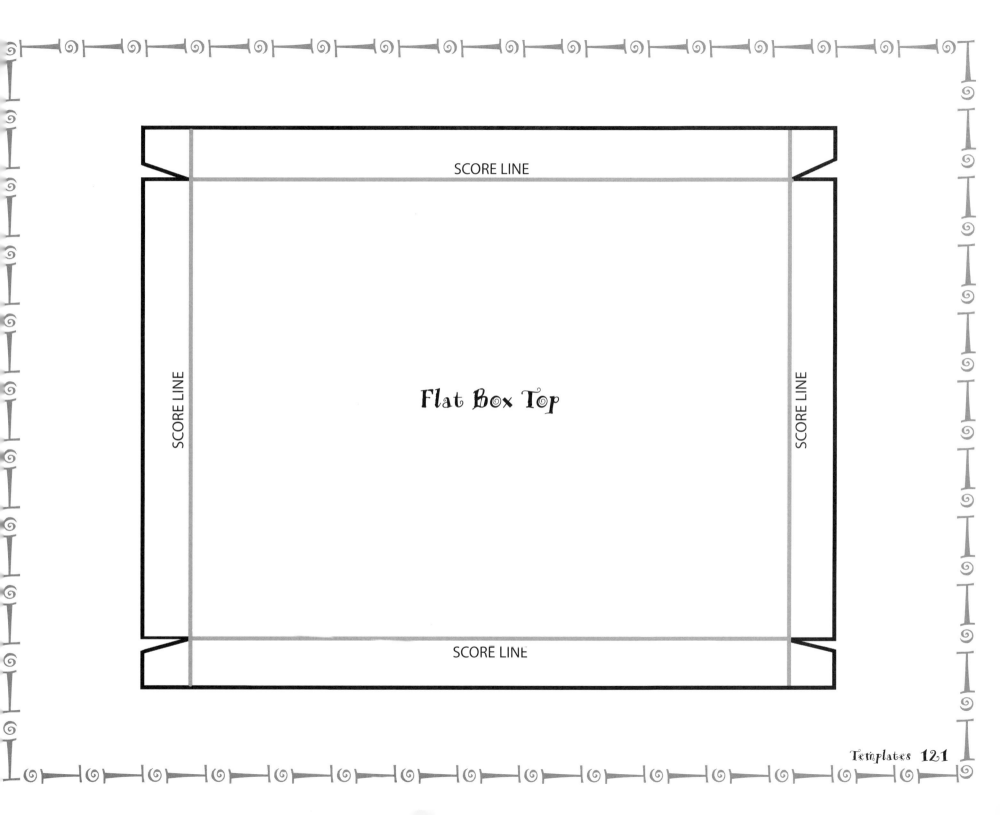

SCORE LINE

SCORE LINE

SCORE LINE

Flat Box Top

SCORE LINE

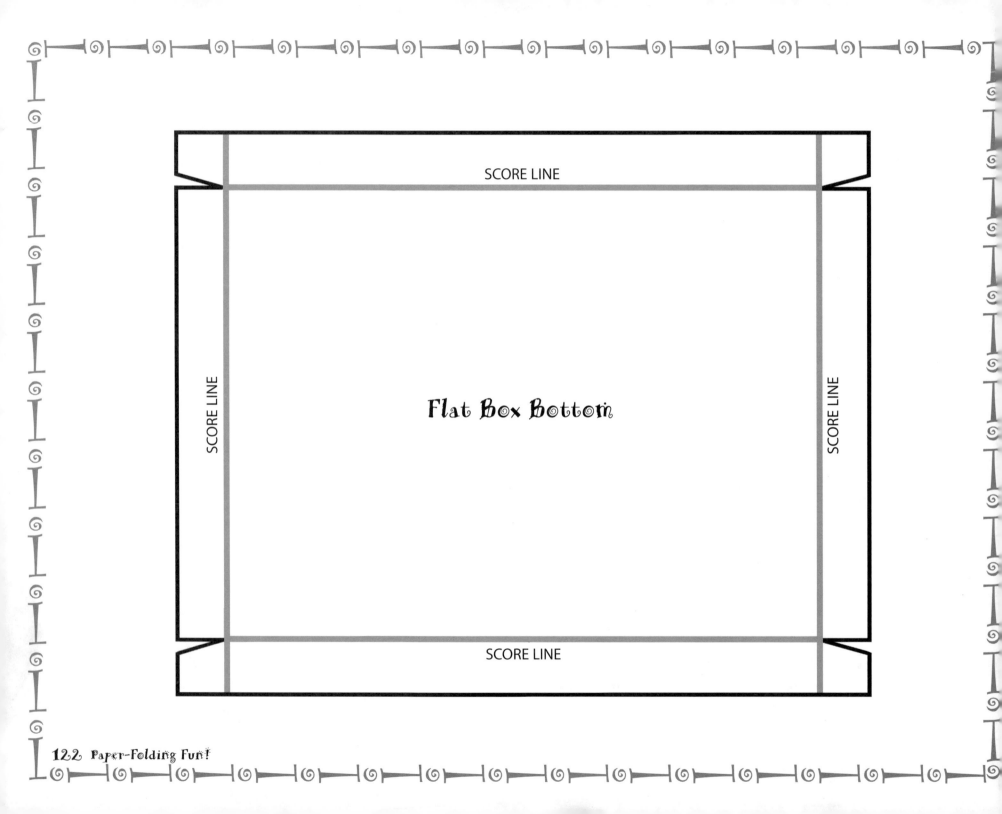

SCORE LINE

SCORE LINE

Flat Box Bottom

SCORE LINE

SCORE LINE

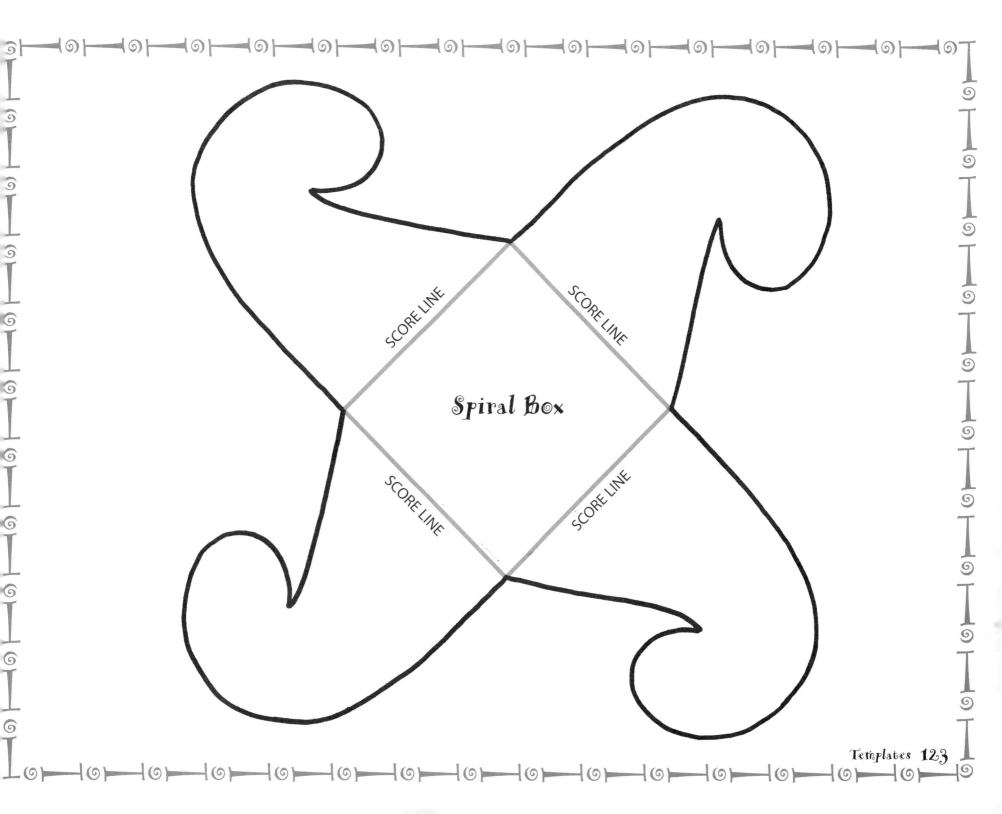

Spiral Box

SCORE LINE

SCORE LINE

SCORE LINE

SCORE LINE

index

More Good Books from Williamson Publishing

Williamson books are available from your bookseller or directly from Williamson Publishing. Please see the next page for ordering information or to visit our website. Thank you.

Other Williamson books by
Ginger Johnson

Make Your Own Christmas Ornaments

Williamson's *Kids Can!*® Books …

Kids Can!® books for ages 6 to 14 are 128 to 176 pages, fully illustrated, trade paper, 11 x 8½, $12.95 US/$19.95 CAN.

Teachers' Choice Award
Dr. Toy Best Vacation Product
CUT-PAPER PLAY!
Dazzling Creations from Construction Paper
by Sandi Henry

Parents' Choice Recommended
KIDS' ART WORKS!
Creating with Color, Design, Texture & More
by Sandi Henry

American Bookseller
  Pick of the Lists
Dr. Toy Best Vacation Product
KIDS' CRAZY ART CONCOCTIONS
50 Mysterious Mixtures for Art & Craft Fun
by Jill Frankel Hauser

Parents' Choice Gold Award
American Bookseller
  Pick of the Lists
THE KIDS' MULTICULTURAL ART BOOK
Art & Craft Experiences from Around the World
by Alexandra M. Terzian

American Booksellers
  Pick of the Lists
Parents' Choice Recommended
ADVENTURES IN ART
Arts & Crafts Experiences for 8- to 13-Year-Olds
by Susan Milord

Benjamin Franklin Best
  Education/Teaching
  Gold Award
Parent's Guide Children's
  Media Award
HAND-PRINT ANIMAL ART
by Carolyn Carreiro
full color, $12.95

Parents' Choice Recommended
The Kids' Guide to MAKING SCRAPBOOKS & PHOTO ALBUMS!
How to Collect, Design, Assemble, Decorate
by Laura Check

JAZZY JEWELRY
Power Beads, Crystals, Chokers, & Illusion and Tattoo Styles
by Diane Baker

Selection of Book-of-the-Month;
Scholastic Book Clubs
KIDS COOK!
Fabulous Food for the Whole Family
by Sarah Williamson and Zachary Williamson

Parents' Choice Gold Award
Benjamin Franklin Best Juvenile
  Nonfiction Award
KIDS MAKE MUSIC!
Clapping and Tapping from Bach to Rock
by Avery Hart and Paul Mantell

American Bookseller
Pick of the Lists
Oppenheim Toy Portfolio
Best Book Award

THE KIDS' SCIENCE BOOK
Creative Experiences for
Hands-On Fun

by Robert Hirschfeld and
Nancy White

Parents' Choice Recommended
THE KIDS' BOOK OF WEATHER
FORECASTING
Build a Weather Station,
"Read" the Sky & Make
Predictions!

with meteorologist Mark Breen
and Kathleen Friestad

Williamson's *Quick Starts for*
***Kids!*™ Books …**

Quick Starts for Kids!™ books for
children, ages 8 and older, are
each 64 pages, fully illustrated,
trade paper, 8 x 10, $7.95
US/$10.95 CAN.

DRAWING HORSES
(that look *real!*)
by Don Mayne

Really Cool
FELT CRAFTS
by Peg Blanchette and
Terri Thibault

GARDEN FUN!
Indoors & Out; In Pots & Small
Spots
by Vicky Congdon

40 KNOTS TO KNOW
Hitches, Loops, Bends &
Bindings
by Emily Stetson

MAKE YOUR OWN FUN
PICTURE FRAMES!
by Matt Phillips

MAKE YOUR OWN HAIRWEAR
Beaded Barrettes, Clips,
Dangles & Headbands
by Diane Baker

Parents' Choice Approved
BAKE THE BEST-EVER
COOKIES!
by Sarah A. Williamson

BE A CLOWN!
Techniques from a Real Clown
by Ron Burgess

Dr. Toy 100 Best Children's
Products
Dr. Toy 10 Best Socially
Responsible Products
MAKE YOUR OWN
BIRDHOUSES & FEEDERS
by Robyn Haus

YO-YO!
Tips & Tricks from a Pro
by Ron Burgess

Oppenheim Toy Portfolio
Gold Award
DRAW YOUR OWN
CARTOONS!
by Don Mayne

KIDS' EASY KNITTING
PROJECTS
by Peg Blanchette

KIDS' EASY QUILTING
PROJECTS
by Terri Thibault

American Bookseller
Pick of the Lists
MAKE YOUR OWN TEDDY
BEARS & BEAR CLOTHES
by Sue Mahren

Visit Our Website

To see what's new at
Williamson and learn more
about specific books, visit
our website at:

www.williamsonbooks.com

To Order Books:

Toll-free phone orders with
credit cards:

1-800-234-8791

We accept Visa and MasterCard
(please include the number and
expiration date).

Or, send a check with your
order to:

Williamson Publishing Company
P.O. Box 185
Charlotte, Vermont 05445

For a free catalog: **mail, phone,**
or **e-mail**

<info@williamsonbooks.com>

Please add **$4.00** for postage for
one book plus **$1.00** for each
additional book. Satisfaction is
guaranteed or full refund without questions or quibbles.